Benedict Kiely

THE IRISH WRITERS SERIES
James F. Carens, General Editor

EIMAR O'DUFFY	Robert Hogan
J. C. MANGAN	James Kilroy
J. M. SYNGE	Robin Skelton
PAUL VINCENT CARROLL	Paul A. Doyle
SEAN O'CASEY	Bernard Benstock
SEUMAS O'KELLY	George Brandon Saul
SHERIDAN LEFANU	Michael Begnal
SOMERVILLE AND ROSS	John Cronin
STANDISH O'GRADY	Phillip L. Marcus
SUSAN L. MITCHELL	Richard M. Kain
W. R. RODGERS	Darcy O'Brien
MERVYN WALL	Robert Hogan
LADY GREGORY	Hazard Adams
LIAM O'FLAHERTY	James O'Brien
MARIA EDGEWORTH	James Newcomer
SIR SAMUEL FERGUSON	Malcolm Brown
BRIAN FRIEL	D. E. S. Maxwell
PEADAR O'DONNELL	Grattan Freyer
DANIEL CORKERY	George Brandon Saul
BENEDICT KIELY	Daniel Casey
CHARLES ROBERT MATURIN	Robert E. Lougy
DOUGLAS HYDE	Gareth Dunleavy
EDNA O'BRIEN	Grace Eckley
FRANCIS STUART	J. H. Natterstad
JOHN BUTLER YEATS	Douglas N. Archibald
JOHN MONTAGUE	Frank Kersnowski
KATHARINE TYNAN	Marilyn Gaddis Rose
BRIAN MOORE	Jeanne Flood
PATRICK KAVANAGH	Darcy O'Brien
OLIVER ST. JOHN GOGARTY	J. B. Lyons
GEORGE FITZMAURICE	Arthur McGuinness

GEORGE RUSSELL (AE)	Richard M. Kain and James H. O'Brien
IRIS MURDOCH	Donna Gerstenberger
MARY LAVIN	Zack Bowen
FRANK O'CONNOR	James Matthews
ELIZABETH BOWEN	Edwin J. Kenney, Jr.
WILLIAM ALLINGHAM	Alan Warner
SEAMUS HEANEY	Robert Buttel
THOMAS DAVIS	Eileen Sullivan

BENEDICT KIELY

Daniel J. Casey

Lewisburg
BUCKNELL UNIVERSITY PRESS
London: Associated University Presses

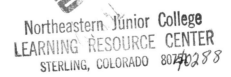

©1974 by Associated University Presses, Inc.

Associated University Presses, Inc.
Cranbury, New Jersey 08512

Associated University Presses
108 New Bond Street
London W1Y OQX, England

Library of Congress Cataloging in Publication Data

Casey, Daniel J   1937–
  Benedict Kiely.

  (The Irish writers series)
  Bibliography: p.
  1.   Kiely, Benedict.
PR6061.I329Z58   828'.9'1409   74–168802
ISBN 0–8387–7936–0
ISBN 0–8387–7970–0 (pbk.)

PRINTED IN THE UNITED STATES OF AMERICA

Contents

Acknowledgments

I should like to thank Benedict Kiely for his many kindnesses over the past two years; for introducing me to Omagh on the banks of the Strule and to the models for many of the characters who appear in his fiction. I thank him, too, for his patience in commenting on chapters of this study and for his permission to quote from the works.

I am also indebted to E. P. Dutton in New York and to Methuen in London for permissions. In Ireland I received special assists from James Delehanty of the *Kilkenny Magazine,* John Ryan of the *Dublin Magazine,* Diarmuid Peavoy of RTE, Bernard Share of *Hibernia,* and from novelist-critic Mervyn Wall. In this country, the assists came from my wife Linda, who diligently checked the manuscript, and from Helen Armour, who typed it.

Chronology

1919   Born August 15 near Dromore, Co. Tyrone, Northern Ireland.
1920   Family moves from Dromore to Omagh.
1936   Completes secondary education at Christian Brothers.
        Employed at Omagh Post Office, 1936–37.
1937   Enters Jesuit novitiate at Emo Park near Portarlington, Co. Laois.
1938   Treated for spinal injury at Cappagh Hospital, Finglas, Co. Dublin.
1939   Returns to Omagh to recuperate and await fall term at University College, Dublin.
1940   Employed by Peter Curry, editor of *The Standard*.
1943   Graduated from National University with B.A. in history and letters.
1944   Marries Maureen O'Connell, July 5.
1945   Journalist, leader writer, and critic for *The Irish Independent*.
        Daughter, Mary Patricia, born.
1946   Anne Kiely, second daughter, born.
1948   Birth of son, John Kiely.
1949   Birth of daughter, Emer Kiely.

1950 Joins *The Irish Press* as literary editor.

1964– Kiely in America; writer-in-residence at Hollins
68   College in Virginia; visiting professor at University of Oregon; writer-in-residence at Emory University in Georgia.

1968 Returns to Ireland.

Benedict Kiely

1

Tom Kiely's Son

Benedict Kiely was born outside of Dromore village in South Tyrone on August 15, 1919, the youngest of six children of Thomas Joseph Kiely and Sarah Alice Gormley. His father, who was born in Moville in County Donegal, took the shilling at eighteen and joined the Leinster Regiment. For some years he traveled in Ireland and abroad, to the Caribbean and to South Africa, where he was decorated for heroism in the Boer War. Tom Kiely was a man to be reckoned with, a man who had, in his time, spoken with De Wet in South Africa, a man who had talked with the wizard Doran on Cornavara Mountain.

And still later he became a chainman on the Ordinance Survey, a job he held until Sarah Alice, the barmaid at Doyle's Hotel in Drumquin, tamed him and persuaded him to accept the saner, more settled life of a family man. The touching story of their courtship and a Holy Thursday cure is thinly masked in Kiely's short story, "Wild Rover No More." In 1920 the former chainman and the manager of James Campbell's Tyrone farm-estate relocated the Kiely family to Omagh

15

and accepted a position as the porter in the new Munster
and Leinster Bank there. Tom Kiely and Sarah Alice
are dead now, though they live on and will continue to
live on in the memories of inhabitants of Omagh and
under various guises in "The White Wild Bronco,"
"Journey to the Seven Streams," "Down Then by
Derry," and in many of Benedict Kiely's longer works.

It is Omagh that he remembers, first, last, and best,
for he is the essential "Omey" man, reared on Gallows
Hill, educated at the Christian Brothers, well-known
and respected yet in all quarters of that County Town.
Kiely reflects:

> All in all it was a good town to grow up in. Thrice happy
> and blessed were the days. The people were friendly and
> fair and as Ulster towns go, not at all given to bigotry.
> They were proud of the town and the rivers, and the valley
> and the moors and mountains above it. Proud of the eigh-
> teenth century courthouse with its Doric face, a building
> once praised by Tyrone Guthrie who said that, if you
> tilted up the long sweep of the High Street and Market
> Street so as to make an auditorium, he could stage a Pas-
> sion Play on the courthouse steps.

Omagh, the town of Mountjoy's forest, the dear native
wildwood and the flowery banks of the serpentine Strule,
was also a garrison town of barracks, and a market
town of shops and stalls and churches. And in "Down
Then by Derry" Kiely dwells on the limping imitation
Gothic spires of Sacred Heart Church and sends a
youngster clambering up the taller one for a panoramic
view of his lovely Strule Valley.

He recalls how his first haircut by Harry the Barber
was given in a unique setting in "A Cow in the House";

he draws on his one-week career at the infant school of
the Loreto Convent in "The Shortest Way Home," and
he confesses other misadventures in and around Omagh
in the stories and novels. His schoolmates and other
boyhood companions—Larry Loughran, Frank Fox,
Tom Tummon, Celsus McCrea, Alex Hyndman, Lanty
and Gerry Cassidy—suggest characters like Aloysius,
the twelve-year-old boarder in "The House in Jail
Square"; Lanty, the accident-prone adventurer who
led an Indian foray into Gormley's Quarries in "The
Wild Boy"; and Andrew Fox, who mixed girls and
greyhounds in "Ten Pretty Girls." And *In a Harbour
Green* he introduces the fifty-nine boys of the Christian
Brothers Choir who had a part in shaping his life and
his writing.

"Homes on the Mountain" is based on the return of
Aunt Rose Gormley McQuaid and her husband to
Dooish Mountain. In the 1930s they arrived back from
Philadelphia to erect an American apartment on the
groundwalls of the cabin where his uncle was born.
Kiely reflects, "Music built the towers of Troy and a
good deal of merriment and malt whiskey went into the
building up there on the mountain where the fields meet
the moor, of as neat a fragment—apart from central
heating—of the American home as you could possibly
imagine." Others of his family, his sisters Rita, Eileen,
and Kathleen, and his brother Gerald (McCartan, a
second brother, died at eight) are also employed as the
models for characters in Kiely's supporting cast.

"A Journey to the Seven Streams" is a delightful
Sunday outing west along the Clanabogan Road from
Omagh. The father hires a chauffeur-driven limousine

to treat the wife and children to a tour of the neighboring townlands. The machine balks regularly at two-mile intervals, and finally on the steep rise between Clanabogan and Cornavara it dies of exhaustion. The excursion cannot be counted a total failure, however, for in it Benedict Kiely presents an elaborate review of local lore, provides a lively exchange among the mother, three sisters, and two brothers, and offers a breathtaking view of the riverine Northern landscape:

> The chief stream came for a long way through soft, deep meadowland. It was slow, quiet, unobtrusive, perturbed only by the movements of water fowl or trout. Two streams met, wonder of wonders, under the arch of a bridge and you could go out under the bridge along a sandy promontory to paddle in clear water on a bottom as smooth as Bundoran strand. Three streams came together in a magic hazel wood where the tiny green unripe nuts were already clustered on the branches. Then the seven made into one, went away from us with a shout and a song towards Shaneragh, Blacksessiagh, Drumragh and Crevenagh, under the humpy crooked King's Bridge where James Stuart had passed on his way from Derry to the fatal brackish Boyne, and on through the town we came from.

Nobody has ever described it better.

Summer holidays meant occasional jaunts to the seaside at Bundoran and a walk toward Finner and the Fairy Bridges, so prominent in "The Fairy Women of Lisbellaw" and in other stories. Or summer holidays would take him to a Gaeltacht college at the Rosses in Donegal, where he polished his Irish and listened intently to the Gaelic storyteller weaving his tales. Or summer holidays would take him to the mountainy sources of the Drumragh and the Camowen, to the quietude of streams, to commune with nature and consider his future.

In 1936, after graduation from secondary school, Kiely found employment at the Omagh Post Office, but in the year following he answered what he thought was a priestly call. He entered the Jesuit novitiate at Emo Park, Portarlington, Co. Laois, and devoted himself to prayer and meditation. In April of 1938, disabled by a tubercular spinal ailment, he was admitted for eighteen months as one of two adult patients at the Cappagh Hospital in Finglas, Co. Dublin. Kiely reflects now that his call to the religious life was in all probability a call to an academic life, and that his convalescence at Cappagh was decisive. The attentions of the pert young nurses drove all thoughts of the priesthood from his mind. In November, 1939, on the eve of World War II, he returned to Omagh to reconsider his future, a future that would see him enroll the following year at the National University in Dublin.

The years 1940–43 were for him banner years, not only did he make lifelong friends at University College, Dublin, but he began a promising career in journalism. Peter O'Curry offered him his first position as a writer on *The Standard,* a Catholic weekly. He met Francis MacManus who gave him encouragement, and he delivered a paper at the Literary Society at U. C. D. that was later published in the *Irish Ecclesiastical Record.* Kiely had the additional good fortune to meet Senan Moynihan, the Kerryman "Friar Tuck," who was a publishing industry in himself, editor of *The Capuchin Annual, Boneventura,* and *The Father Matthew Record.* Senan printed sev-

eral of Kiely's poems in *Boneventura* and accepted both
"Long After O'Neill" and "Journey in Ulster," the
second written by Kiely under the pseudonym Conal
Casey, for the 1943 *Annual*.

By the time of graduation in 1943 Benedict Kiely was
well on his way to becoming an established writer in the
City of Writers, and a year later, when he married
Maureen O'Connell, he had taken a second step from
Omagh. After a brief stint of graduate studies in history
at University College, Dublin, Kiely produced his first
book-length work, *Counties of Contention: A Study of the
Origin and Implications of Partition* (1945). The treatise, published by Mercier Press in Cork, excited great furor
among Nationalists who found the author an eloquent
spokesman for their cause and among Unionists who
considered it altogether exasperating. That same year
Kiely accepted a position as leader writer and literary
critic for *The Irish Independent*.

Land without Stars, (1946) the first novel, was followed
by a succession of the better-known novels: *In a Harbour
Green* (1949), *Call for a Miracle* (1950), *Honey Seems Bitter*
(1952), *The Cards of the Gambler* (1953), *There Was an Ancient
House* (1955), and *The Captain with the Whiskers* (1960).
Methuen published an excellent short story collection,
A Journey to the Seven Streams: Seventeen Stories in 1963. There
were, along the way, two highly acclaimed critical vol-
umes, *Poor Scholar: A Study of William Carleton (1794–1869)*
and *Modern Irish Fiction—A Critique* (1950), and a raft of
stories, articles, and reviews for numerous periodicals.

By 1950 Kiely, now the father of three, had succeeded
M. J. MacManus as literary editor of *The Irish Press*,
a post that he held until 1964, when he left Ireland for

America. As literary editor, he knew nearly every writer of fiction, every literary critic, and every major work to appear in Ireland for more than a generation, and those critics who knew the scene as well as he, heralded Kiely's fiction as exceptional.

In 1964 Benedict Kiely accepted an invitation from Hollins College in Virginia to become writer-in-residence there. In 1965 he journeyed west to be professor in creative writing at the University of Oregon, and from 1966–68 he was in residence at Emory University in Atlanta, Georgia. Meanwhile his "Letters from America" appeared regularly in *The Irish Times,* and his stories, articles, and criticism were featured in leading American periodicals and reviews. *The Irish Times* "Letters" catalogued the writer's impressions of American regional idiosyncracies and provided alternately hilarious and somber insights into the American psyche. The *New Yorker* stories continued to appear but there were several others in periodicals like *Kenyon Review, Texas Quarterly,* and *Northwest Review.* His article, entitled "Thanksgiving in the Hoosegow," in *Nation* examined Southern justice, tongue in cheek, and the criticism in *The New York Times Book Review* came to be valued by both editors and readers.

Kiely decided by 1968 that he had been too long away from Dublin, and he returned home in time to release his eighth and most important novel, *Dogs Enjoy the Morning,* published by Victor Gollancz. Since 1968 he has continued to write special features for *The Irish Times,* make occasional radio and television appearances, and present lectures in literature at U. C. D. His short fiction is found in the pages of the *New Yorker,* his reviews in

The New York Times, and in other reputable American and Irish periodicals. "Down Then by Derry," the finest short story to date, appeared in the *Dublin Magazine* in 1970, and Gollancz issued his second successful collection, *A Ball of Malt and Madame Butterfly: A Dozen Stories,* in 1973. His works-in-progress include two Northern novels, *Nothing Ever Happens at Carmincross* and *A Question of Language,* and *A Pictorial History of the Irish People.* There are, of course, many more stories to be told.

2

The Instinct and the Art

Irish writers have made significant contributions to modern fiction, yet it is a *seanachie's* voice that can be heard in the work of some of the most accomplished of them. It is unmistakable in the stories of Frank O'Connor, Sean O'Faolain, Liam O'Flaherty, and others of the breed; it is unmistakable in the stories of Benedict Kiely.

Kiely admits to sometimes hearing a Gaelic folksinger accompanied by the wind in the bushes and the waves on shore, and he sometimes imagines himself rendering his tales in a sort of splendid isolation in a Gaeltacht cottage with fires dancing shadows off the walls. Nearly every story seems to revive a forgotten melody, nearly every one is played against the wail of Uilleann pipes. He reminds us, "But in Ireland the man attempting to shape the present by looking back into or listening attentively to the past runs the risk of becoming the victim of a perpetual meeting and agreement and disagreement of opposites, hears one voice telling of beauty and another voice wailing of death, one voice shouting in joy and another voice creaking with bitterness." He also reminds us that in Ireland living in both

worlds is commonplace. The Irish novelist concerned
with presenting his society as it is ignores the weight of
tradition and the sense of history at his peril. To a greater degree than even he would perhaps admit, the content
and technique of Kiely's fiction are dictated by a voice
out of the past.

To what extent is the modern Irish story an instinctive
response to the glowing hearth and to what extent is it
conscious art? Could it be that the ancient narrative
with its intricacies and its compound standards is, after
all, the more complicated and the more demanding aesthetically? For more than thirty years Kiely has stood
with one foot in the past and the other in the present,
mingling joys and disappointments of the two worlds,
and, so postured, he has managed to create a fiction
that is more than credible; it is convincing.

Since 1940 Kiely's criticism has appeared in *The Standard, The Independent, The Press,* and *The Irish Times.* Every
major journal in Ireland has carried his appreciations,
critical articles, and reviews, and Radio Telefis Eireann
has broadcast his fame as one of Ireland's important
literary voices. In Britain and the United States Kiely
is, of course, best known for the creative work. He does,
however, contribute criticism on Irish fare to *The New
York Times Book Review* on occasion, and he has been
invited to submit to trans-Atlantic literary symposia,
like the *Kenyon Review* series on short fiction and David
Madden's excellent *Rediscoveries* collection. What is perhaps most significant about Kiely's criticism is that it
responds to the work directly and genuinely, that it
ignores the author's origin, education, and prior efforts,
as it ignores the commentary of literary historians and

contemporary reviewers. Kiely is his own man; he is informed, articulate, and independent, and his literary views are valued by discriminating editors at home and abroad.

In 1947 Sheed and Ward published a long overdue study of the controversial nineteenth-century Tyrone novelist, William Carleton. Kiely's biographical-critical volume was a labor of love for the writer he called "the greatest novelist that Ireland in the nineteenth century gave to the English language." In fact, the study was to be of immense importance to both Carleton and Kiely.

William Carleton emerged from the Tyrone cabins where Irish was spoken and became the folk-historian of pre-Famine Ireland. In his sketches of weddings, dances, wakes and in his graphic descriptions of famine, eviction, and emigration, Carleton depicted a score of memorable characters and preserved customs and beliefs that might otherwise have perished with the folk. Yeats called him an historian, but he was an historian only in the sense that he reported "what people say to each other on fair days and high days, and in how they farm, and quarrel, and go on pilgrimage." Ben Kiely understood Carleton as he understood Yeats's fondness for Carleton, and he understood how and why Carleton's fiction was superior to the fiction of Maria Edgeworth, John Banim, and Gerald Griffin. To Carleton he awarded the *seanachie's* place in nineteenth-century fiction, for Carleton presided over the hearth, alternating amusing and terrifying tales that were unequaled in strength, unparalleled in authenticity, tales born in the Tyrone cottages and along the Irish country roads and written later in

Traits and Stories. Ben Kiely appreciated Carleton's importance as few others did, and he set about adding a
few pages to Irish literary history.

What was particularly refreshing was that Kiely's
view was not the trite, jaundiced view of the Catholic
critic injured or incensed by Carleton's early propagan-
distic fiction. The *Christian Examiner* sketches, edited by
that "lean controversialist" Caesar Otway, were mis-
shapen diatribes against what Otway called "Romish
superstitions." Carleton has been accused of wavering
on the political and religious issues, but there is reason
to believe that his wavering was prompted by sincere
doubts. If Carleton's conversion to the Church of Ireland was genuine and his politics were reactions against
the excesses that assuredly existed in evil days, should
he have been misrepresented, maligned, and finally cast
aside? *Poor Scholar* plays down the doctrinal biases and
historical inaccuracies, though they certainly influenced
Carleton's life and his literary outlook. Instead, Kiely
speaks to stylistic faults, to the author's propensity for
moralizing, to his cumbrous prose passages, to his
penchant for reducing potential tragedy to the level of
melodrama. The truth of the matter is that Carleton's
fiction is quite uneven; it runs the gamut from the superb
well-wrought narratives of *sgéalaí* to the stilted wood-
en homilies of the country pedant.

What Kiely read was the history of the neighboring
valleys in which he and Carleton were reared, and what
he heard was the lore of the place. He understood better
than the others the apparent contradiction that followed
Carleton all the days of his life; he also recognized
Carleton's exceptional skill as a teller of tales. He pre-

sents Carleton, then, not as an opportunist, a double agent for Otway or Gavan Duffy, but as a writer of passionate intensity who saw man's capacity for good and evil and who represented both natures in his fiction. And he portrays him sympathetically as the great peasant, tormented by the poverty, ignorance, greed, superstition, and by the sectarian hatreds and rivalries prevalent in the Ireland of his day.

As Carleton needed Ben Kiely, so Kiely owed a debt to him. In *Poor Scholar* the young writer was sounding his own depths; he was beginning to realize that there were remarkable parallels between his subject and himself. Hadn't Kiely come out of the neighboring valley? Hadn't he the same aspirations as Carleton—the priesthood, the university, and literature? Hadn't he walked the same rivers, traveled the same hills, and taken that same rocky road to Dublin a century later? And hadn't Benedict Kiely decided, more than a century later, that his own fiction was meant to open a window on the soul of his people? He had resolved to carry on the legacy that Carleton had left him.

With the publication of *Poor Scholar* Kiely achieved what Yeats could not. In 1889 W. B. Yeats edited his *Stories From Carleton*, where he dubbed Carleton "the greatest novelist of Ireland by right of the most Celtic eyes that ever gazed from under the brow of story-teller." The volume was poorly received. Yeats failed to revive an interest in Carleton, and what's more, he failed to awaken even scholarly concern. Since the 1947 publication of *Poor Scholar*, Carleton's autobiography and works have been republished, *Poor Scholar* has been reprinted, and a great many scholarly articles have appeared in

the learned journals. *Poor Scholar* is Ben Kiely's testament
of faith in William Carleton, but it is more than that.
It is itself a well-wrought, reinterpretation of a deliberately neglected nineteenth-century novelist, a tribute
to Kiely's critical persuasion and a belated tribute to
Carleton's significance as a writer of prose fiction.

With *Poor Scholar* behind him, Ben Kiely turned to a
more ambitious and precarious subject, a survey of
Irish fiction from World War I to mid-century. The
volume, segments of which had appeared in the *Irish
Bookman,* or had been broadcast as reviews for Radio
Éireann covered thirty-two years and included more than
fifty writers.

Kiely's postscript to the work suggested that this
comprehensive survey attempted too much, that a
selective survey might have been more advantageous.
The years 1918-1950 were, after all, the prolific years in
Irish fiction, years in which Joyce, O'Connor, O'Faolain,
O'Flaherty, Stephens, Beckett, and Flann O'Brien
wrote prodigious works. There was an added problem—
a critique of fifty contemporaries in a country as small
and incestuous as Ireland might bring imprecations
eternal on the critic and his line. Kiely had to contend
not only with Joyce and Company, but also with Eliz-
abeth Bowen, Daniel Corkery, Michael McLaverty,
Kate O'Brien, and Francis Stuart, and those in the
young-but-promising class, like Mary Lavin, Walter
Macken, and Bryan MacMahon. That he managed to
complete the survey amidst the flurry of publication
and that his judgments on the major writers have been
substantiated time and again by subsequent criticism is
a credit to his discretion and his literary vision.

In advance of the surge of Joyce criticism Kiely summed up the creator and the *Wake* in these words:

> Joyce pressed the work into one volume by an unprecedented feat of condensation, by making an attempt to join together a hundred words so as to make not another word but an all-significant harmony. As a record of mankind the book is very likely a failure, because of that doubtful cyclic theory of history, because Joyce, being a great laugher and not a philosophic historian, being also a pedant, buried his meaning under a million pedantries and a million puns.

He dissected the master punster and myth-maker with disarming ease and showed a conversance with Joycean techniques that has been limited to a few perspicacious critics and a few great laughers.

He pays homage to Sean O'Faolain for his undisputed mastery in the short story. "There is smoothness and grace in the actual writing; there is a preference for the significant moment which is frequently a contemplative moment and is more important for O'Faolain—and for any wise man—than the platform called plot or the unreality called a central character," says Kiely, adding that life has no central characters. He speaks of O'Flaherty's attention to environment, to his use of birds and beasts and myths and legends. And despite O'Flaherty's shouting to prove himself the harshest of realists, Kiely regards him a wild Aran romantic enveloped in defiant dreams. He examines Frank O'Connor as well, and credits him with a deft artistry, with telling his stories so that they fairly hum with speed, excitement, and laughter. Yet Kiely attributes O'Connor's success to his fascination for ordinary people engaged in ordinary activity.

Considering O'Faolain, O'Flaherty, and O'Connor, Kiely displays the respect of a journeyman for a trades- man, but one senses too, an almost filial affection for the trinity of master storytellers under whom he has served a soul apprenticeship. In Kiely's fiction there are the same significant moments, the smoothness and grace, the use of birds and beasts and myths and legends. In Kiely's fiction there are ordinary people and children, and there is a sense that the fellow telling the story en- joys the speed, excitement, and laughter, as much as his reader does. "What is Irish fiction but a personal emo- tion woven into the general pattern of myth and legend," Kiely muses.

The sharp observations in *Modern Irish Fiction* are not limited to Joyce, O'Faolain, O'Flaherty, and O'Connor, however. Kiely says of James Stephens that he "could have seen wonderful things through that mountain furze; he might even have seen the gods." He says "Francis Stuart is as important as a novelist as Jack B. Yeats is a painter." He calls Seamus O'Kelly's "The Weaver's Grave," the unsung masterpiece in Irish fiction. Kiely displays always a sharp critical eye offering a great many right judgments on the period fare. The writers of 1918– 1950 are all in *Modern Irish Fiction,* their novels and stories scrutinized by the skillful critic and accomplished prac- titioner. Sean McMahon, in a 1966 *Eire-Ireland* piece, called the book, "the best and most detailed survey of Irish writing since 1920."

Perhaps *Modern Irish Fiction* is, after all, too compre- hensive and perhaps it does suffer the deficiencies of like criticism, as Kiely suggests, but he need not be apologetic for the matter or method. In this survey he has exhibited candor, tact, and familiarity, a literary sophistication beyond his years. He has provided, in its pages, the only comprehensive study of the most important period in Irish fiction and defined qualities of excellence in the modern Irish prose narrative.

"Take what you see out of life," Kiely told a group of aspiring young writers at Listowel in 1972, "and shape it in the imagination; it is not what happened but what should have happened that is important." The writer takes the position that remembering is the beginning of the novelist's business, but he insists that it is only the beginning. There is not only the experience and the memory of the experience, but the imagination that moves it forward, and then the inexplicable mystery of art.

"When I first read *Moby Dick* I thought it was about a one-legged man chasing a white whale," he tells his reader. Kiely looks with suspicion on involved symbolism, and he frequently rebukes scholars for reading too much into a novel. Yet he neither mitigates his own dependence on symbols nor defends his preference for Hawthorne, Poe, and Faulkner. He is symbolist, allegorist, and myth maker, and his fiction employs ambiguity, paradox, irony, satire—whatever device serves to heighten involvement at the moment. His writing is influenced by naturalism and existentialism on the Continent and by the psychological novelists of Britain and the United States. He might have been a realist, a naturalist, some sort of avant-garde experimentalist, but he has too much imagination to be any of those. Surely he is one of the last of the Irish romantics but with an abiding fascination for the darker side of man's nature. Imagination over-

whelms reality, and myth and legend introduce a new
level of consciousness to his work. He cannot avoid
blending the strange and the real, adding song and poetry, or embellishing his landscape with a rich flow of
images that stir scenes replete with illusions.

From his stories of the late forties and early fifties to
those of the seventies, one notes a definite progression
in Kiely's narrative complexity. The early fiction offers
relatively uncomplicated incidents, stories told in the
first person or stories told omnisciently, but with a distinct sense of the narrator's presence. The later fiction
is, by contrast, more subtle, more suggestive, darker and
more complex. While they seem to lack narrative unity,
the later stories move in loose psychological streams
that have a tendency to keep doubling back on one another, melding in a single cumulative effect.

"Blackbird in a Bramble Bough," Kiely's earliest
published story, appeared in the *Irish Bookman* in Septem-
ber, 1946. It is rather direct—the narrator examines the
photo of a poet in a Philadelphia newspaper that is sent
to a local publican. (He was the first poet he ever knew.)
He reads the American critic's comment on the poetry;
"a note of freshness like the song of the blackbird on a
bramble bough," it says. Then he reflects on the poet
and the incident that brought the celebrity and him together for one memorable evening not many months
before.

The narrator recalls, too, how he came to be at the
lecture on Alice Meynell at the *aula maxima* in the convent
school—a guest invitation from a seminarian cousin. He
vividly recollects the bald, obese poet of the clammy
hand, the Chestertonian cape, and the book-and-bottle-

laden grip. That night the young narrator's speculations were far from the words of the caped wonder, the poetry of dear dead Alice, or the tea and sweetcakes offered by the withered nun from Waterford. He fantasized instead about the soft white feminine loveliness lined row on row before him; he exchanged knowing glances with a golden-haired lass, and he imagined frothy pints and congenial company in the town below.

The young man becomes the custodian of the distinguished visitor whom he comes quickly to despise. After transporting poet and valise to the hotel and standing more rounds than he should, the narrator succeeds in sending the drunken muse staggering through the rear gates of the convent garden in search of other after-hours pleasures. The episode is more than mildly amusing; it is told well enough that the author selected it for inclusion in his collection, *A Journey to the Seven Streams,* seventeen years later.

The early short fiction, "Blackbird in the Bramble Bough" (1946), "The King's Shilling" (1947), "The Pilgrims" (1950), and "Rich and Rare Were the Gems She Wore" (1951), and the early novels were straightforward narratives. They were sometimes flawed by contrived situations, by characters that were stereotyped, and by unnecessarily elaborate descriptions, but the flaws were overbalanced by numerous imaginative incidents, convincing characters, and fine lyrical passages. Kiely's language is a strange blend of poetic inversions, fragments, and rambling, adjective-weighted sentences in the early writings, but the dialogue is good, good enough to make them twice readable. If the early fiction is uneven and if it tends toward the conventional, the stories themselves, and particularly "Rich and Rare Were the Gems She Wore," still fare better than most other fiction of the period.

Twelve years after he wrote of the first poet he ever knew, Kiely spins a wistful yarn that perfectly contrasts the imaginary and real. "The White Wild Bronco" (1958) is the first of his many *New Yorker* stories. Isaac's child view of the world from a creepie stool is markedly different from his invalid father's horizontal perspective. Yet, as the town gathers around the invalid father's bedside to hear him read the nightly instalments of "Tarzan and the Apes," imagination shuts out reality, and romanticism triumphs for the moment.

At first Isaac's microcosm extends slightly beyond the recognition of a devoted mother standing attendance at the heroic remnant of his bedridden father. It is a small world populated by Doherty, the stout undertaker; Mickey Fish, the girl-crazy herringmonger; Pat Moses Gavigan, pike fisher and blackthorn sculptor; and Cowboy Carson, cowpuncher, wagoner, and stacker of grain. Beyond the bedroom world there are, of course, other dreamers and realists: Attention Dale, the stargazing grainmerchant; Tansey, the tightfisted carter, and his six hefty sisters; and the Taggarts, horse traders from the Connacht gypsy camps.

Isaac's cottage, snug in the middle of a terrace of seven white cottages, looks out on a bustling Northern town of shops, warehouses, and railway yards. The hospital is nearby at the salmon leap on the Camowen River and greater distance is measured in miles to the Blacksessiagh. But Isaac's child world of Devlin's Sweetie Shop and his vision of Tarzan, Jane, and the Maoris begin to fade with the passing years. He has outgrown the creepie stool. Kiely interrupts his narrative to recall Isaac for his listeners. He was that fine young boxer who brought medals, cups, belts, and other trophies back to this town just before the war. The invalid fusilier's son . . . a natural champion . . . a man among men.

There are, besides Isaac, two men that Kiely studies closely in "The White Wild Bronco." There was the heroic fusilier, who was marched home from the war stomachless in a glass case after having led an advance on his own artillery. To him reality was a bed and a memory. And there was Cowboy Carson, whose gun duels with Wyatt Earp spilled out of Deadwood Dick pulp westerns into his own lackluster existence. So it was that Edgar Rice Burroughs offered the fusilier a respite from savage memories of the battlefield, and the pulp authors provided an escape for a would-be Irish cowpoke. Somewhere between lush African jungle growth and lawless Dodge City, there was a reality that was perhaps too awesome and too stark.

Isaac's wish for a pony led him to Tansey's livery yard, where he first gazed on the white wild bronco from Ballinasloe. It seemed as if the white limbed stallion would never be broken; it had the savage spirit of Tarzan and Wyatt Earp combined. Isaac's fascination for the bronc never waned until the day the carter struck the beast a blow between the eyes with a crowbar and drove the spirit out of him. It was that very day that the fusilier destroyed his young son's faith in Cowboy Carson's Rio Grande exploits, the day that reality silenced his imagination.

By the time Isaac had gone off to war against the

Germans, the invalid fusilier had been laid to rest by Doherty, and stargazing, girl-watching, and the carving of blackthorns were less-prized arts. Only Cowboy Carson refused to vacate the imaginary world: he would relive Deadwood Dick's western feats with the compassionate Yank soldiers en route to the French battlefields. Isaac was killed at the Rhine crossing, but the storyteller assures us that he remained until then "the best fighter our town ever had."

"The White Wild Bronco" crackles with irony and humor throughout. The child Isaac, asked what he would be when he grew up, stutters "a German," and the Germans take his life. The invalid hero in the big bed, who was shot by his own guns, is visited on British Legion days by the Bloodless Lady Haig. And in the end only Cowboy Carson's world of fantasy survives intact. Isaac's progress had been charted from infancy to an early grave. But Kiely's attraction for his Ulster childhood and his youthful companions extends beyond a single cottage and a single tale. The well-wrought boyish tales of adventure, the *New Yorker* stories of 1958–62 vintage, recapture the innocence and mischief of the author's youth in and around Omagh, and his wit, at times subtle, more often rollicking, lends a Celtic madness to each sketch.

Twelve years after "The White Wild Bronco" and twenty-four years after "Blackbird in a Bramble Bough," Benedict Kiely offers what may well be his best short fiction, in a 1970 *Dublin Magazine* piece, "Down Then by Derry." The narrator begins with an apparent digression: "The first time Tom Cunningham saw Sadie Law's brother, Francie, that brother was airborne between the saddle of a racing bicycle and a stockade filled with female lunatics." He confesses, in the next breath, that neither Francie nor his sister is to be the chief character in "Down Then by Derry," but he fulfills an obligation to explain Francie's aerial predicament. In fact, Sadie Law and Tom Cunningham are two of a large supporting cast in the loose-knit narrative that shifts between the "now" and the "then."

The middle-aged traveler returns, after an absence of thirty years, to his Northern hometown, dominated by a Catholic church with hopalong spires. He is accompanied by a clever, quizzical sixteen-year-old daughter and a no less curious fourteen-year-old son. As the trio ascend and descend the High Street into the Market Street, the father revives once-upon-a-time characters and events. The haunting verses of an Omagh poem meanwhile play upon his consciousness:

> Thrice happy and blest were the days of my childhood,
> And happy the hours I wandered from school
> By green Mountjoy's forest our dear native wildwood
> And the green flowery banks of the serpentine Strule.

His octogenarian mother tells the children how their father was always fond of quoting poetry. The kitchen palaver continues, but he soon lapses into a reverie of Gothic spires overlooking the riverine beauty of the Strule, youthful caresses on hillside, and that song that whispered of the history of the place and the fate of the Gaelic woodsmen of Tyrone. The reverie spills into the momentary reality of a grave—his father's grave—but the relics of things past and the children's queries prompt memory again and again. Images of Sadie Law,

Tom Cunningham, Angela Brown, an exiled woman in Wisconsin, the lady of Glenshrule are revived between the insistent verses of that poem. "Down Then by Derry" runs present, past, and distant past together, employing the cinematic effects of fading, blending, and continuous flashing back and forward to produce a unity of effect.

The ancient woodsmen, axes on shoulders, speaking a guttural language doomed to die, abandoned the town to the prosperous English-speaking townsmen and shop-keepers, as Angela abandoned the narrator for a fusilier named Nixon. Tom Cunningham never returned home after the war. The exile in Wisconsin remembered clearly from a distance, and the fair lady of Glenshrule drank herself beyond oblivion when her brothers followed the well-worn route to Derry and the sea.

The beauty of Benedict Kiely's later stories does not rest solely on his talent for skillfully manipulating three levels of life and three levels of history, or in recreating the loveliness of that serpentine Strule. He also revives the country customs—an aged mother who spat slightly and politely into fire or handkerchief when the devil was mentioned and who paid her debts before the new year began; a feast that sent young pagans climbing Slieve Drumond to pluck blayberries and insure local fertility. There are the humorous diversions, as well. The author combines the perfection of a complex narrative technique with lovely poetic description, and he elicits a feeling of nostalgia that is surely heightened by comic relief.

If Kiely has been criticized for pedantry, elaborate description, and lack of narrative unity, such criticism is out of place for these later stories. Every phrase, indeed every word, contributes to the artistry of the piece. Here Kiely is the master of understatement, and when he tells his reader that Sadie Law was almost as famous as her brother, but not for track cycling, there is no mistake about the entendre. "Embrocation" takes on special desirable significance in this story. The *ubi sunt* motif is inherent in the author's use of the "Down Then by Derry" poem, the melancholy stanzas of which punctuate segments of the story. In the end Sadie Law, sixtyish and wearing the uniform of the hotel staff, comes from the kitchen to exchange memories and shake hands. She tells the traveler how Francie the cyclist has been confined to a chair since he broke his back in a racing accident years ago.

Memory tries to alter truth but truth has a way of intruding itself. The puzzle of the past and the distant past begins to make sense, and the returnee confides to his children: "But once upon a time I laughed easily. It was easy to laugh here then." "Down Then by Derry" is in the complex mode of Kiely's later fiction, a fiction that harkens back to the "thrice happy and blest" years of childhood, a fiction that frequently contrasts youth and maturity.

In "A Room in Linden," a 1972 *New Yorker* story, history lives along the cold green corridors of the old manse and it lives in the memories of the aged convalescents. The Boer War veteran, the vaudevillian with shaking paralysis, and the crochety priest-historian are damned to an eternal December. The loud cry in the night tells the young seminarian that the bawdy soldier has finally fought and lost. The entertainer suffers a stroke that renders him speechless, and the old priest confesses that he is already dead to his religious community.

The young invalid reflects that one must look back to a new conquest, a new stage, a new book to see heaven. "Heaven, like most things, doesn't last, or could only be an endless repetition of remembered happinesses, and in the end be, like dying, a bloody bore." As he sits in a shady corner of a public park, watching a reclining girl cycling to the moon, the strong legs of the tennis players, and a red-haired footballer, the young man says, "So everybody is happy and the park is beautiful." Even if he must return to the house of the dead and to his room in Linden, it will only be for a short time.

"Down Then by Derry," "A Room in Linden," and his most recent story, "An Old Friend," are reminiscences of a life well spent but with further philosophical speculations on the meaning of life and death. They look back romantically on days gone and on friends fading; they are impossible dreams that can only be answered by more dreams.

Over the years Benedict Kiely's fiction has been consistently good, aesthetically superior. The early stories had occasional flaws; the later ones showed a marked stylistic development and perfection of narrative skill. Through all of the writing there is, however, a dependence on biographical and historical references. Not that he has striven for faithful representation of character, place, or event; he has, in fact, transformed the landscape and consciously altered history, legend, and lore to fit his design. Kiely's art is a conscious art. But there is, too, an awareness we have in reading him that at times his story outgrows the printed page and has the author in its grip. The *seanachie's* instinct is so compelling that he has to resist it intentionally if he is to stay beyond its grasp. Instead, he delights in stepping out of the shadows, sizing up the audience, putting an ember in his pipe, and opening the story in a resonant Ulster brogue.

Benedict Kiely combines the best of the traditional and the modern. He is important on the current Irish literary scene—important for his novels and short stories and important for his continuous influence on modern Irish criticism. He is probably the first to credit his success as a writer to Carleton, Yeats, Joyce, O'Connor, O'Flaherty, O'Faolain, Beckett, and Stephens and to his extensive involvement with Russian, French, English, and American literatures; and to his participation in the rich folk tradition of his native Tyrone. But there is more to it than that. He is immensely talented, a gifted writer with an unfettered imagination. He comes to us an apt pupil, an able critic, and a conscious artist, whose contribution to Irish fiction and criticism have been universally acknowledged, whose fuller contribution to Irish writing lies ahead.

3

Ballyclogher to Dublin: The Early Novels, 1946–1950

Benedict Kiely's first novel appeared one year after *Counties of Contention,* an uncomprising analysis of the incidents that led to the partitioning of Ireland in 1921. The reality of the border and the realities of the writer's Nationalist breeding and background inevitably intrude on fiction set in a province torn by factionalism and war. *Land without Stars* takes place, he tells us, in an Ireland "divided by a political boundary into two fragments, the smaller of which is misnamed 'Ulster,' the larger misnamed 'Eire.'" During the eight- or nine-month period of the story, Republicanism continues a threat to the Six Counties, and the North becomes party to Britain's War against Hitler.

Border conflict and the impact of the World War on a Northern market and garrison town account for unusual external tensions and heighten the psychological struggles of two brothers with conflicting ideologies. The novel moves through the lush river-rich Strule Valley of Tyrone, along the winding country roads, and into Ballyclogher and a hilly town of tumbled uneven roofs with a domed courthouse and town hall, a divided town whose Catholic imitation-Gothic spires dwarf the plain steeple of the Protestant church, a bustling town with an active British military complement. It moves, too, into the rugged terrain of the Donegal mountains and seacoast—to the primitive Gaeltacht of the Rosses and Aranmore. Kiely introduces his reader to an Ulster that is culturally bleeding and politically broken by the petty rivalries of Irish, British, and Germans, and he laments her fate with all of the passion of the seventeenth-century Gaelic poet.

The title is from Egan O'Rahilly's "Concerning the Destruction of the Great Families," an elegy that signals the beginning of the end. The bitter poet sang of

A land poor, afflicted, lonely, and tortured!
A land without a husband, without a son, without a spouse!
A land without vigour, or spirit, or hearing!
A land in which no justice is to be done to the poor!

A land without produce or thing of worth of any kind!
A land without dry weather, without a stream, without a star!
A land stripped naked, without shelter or boughs!
A land broken down by the English-prating band!

But there was no God to deliver the Gaels from the scourge of the English invasions in O'Rahilly's day and no God to deliver Ireland now. The novelist looks back angrily to the seventeenth-century demise of the Gaelic order, to the time when the Irish dream became an Irish nightmare.

Land without Stars is first the psychological study of a young man caught in a spiritual dilemma. Peter Quinn's soul searching, his anxiety at repudiating a call to the priesthood and finding a way to confess his "failure" publicly, is traumatic. Mrs. Quinn's insistence that "God needs good priests," and Peter's abiding guilt in disappointing "a good mother who prayed that her son might go forward to the altar of God" underline that sense of failure. The clerical privileges extended to him by lady parishioners, taximen, customs officials, and friends underline it, too. Peter had, after all, broken his word to God in rejecting the eternal celibacy of the priesthood and in choosing a physical love twice denied him. His cynicism becomes a refuge for his failure and his brooding emanates from a sense of guilt as much as it does from a sense of failure.

Peter is the intelligent, courageous *literatus* who tries the will of God with a "Non serviam" not prompted by pride. His refusal to countenance violent extremist views is conscionable, for the town with the curious slanting eyes peering from ancient doorways is the town that has also profaned the tradition: "This was Ireland, as absurd and entangled as the whole lunatic world, each man like each nation, digging into the past for buried bitterness to anger him against his neighbor." Peter can make the essential distinctions between the outlaw who murders without a cause and the well-meaning rebel whose dreams somehow run askew, and while he values the old songs, poetry, and stories, as well as the language that enshrines them, he values them as positive inheritances. He is not the spoiled poet, even if he is the spoiled priest. His vision is clear, his logic irrefutable.

Davy Quinn is incorrigible; he is Peter's antithesis, an incurable romantic out of the pages of O'Casey. But because he is one of the indomitable Irishry, we respond sympathetically to his idealism. In the end Davy has sacrificed everything, dark Rita Keenan, his freedom, and his life. And Rita's plight, like Davy's, requires courage, for ultimately she must be prepared to answer to Davy and to their families and to the community for her actions.

There are well-drawn minor characters as well. Mr. Quinn is a postman and a British army veteran of the Boer War whose irascible temperament has mellowed with the years. Over Christmas dinner he reviews the boyhood scenes of priest hunts and evictions and tales of smugglers, tinkers, and lunatics. Mrs. Quinn is a patient, self-sacrificing Irish mother, and Mary, her daughter, the steadying influence in the home. There are, too, Jim Carson, the Republican schoolteacher; and Pete and Jacob, the aged bachelors whose hut becomes a refuge for IRA men; and Dick Slevin, the sinister gunman.

Land without Stars is, in many respects, impressive, and as Kiely's first novel, a consideration of it is critically important to establishing narrative techniques, stylistic influences, and the early themes. It is an uncomplicated psychological novel of multiplying contrasts that examines human strength and weakness with honesty and compassion. The author shifts easily from third-person narrator with Peter as sentient center to first-person narrator with Davy and Peter reflecting on their innermost thoughts and feelings and addressing the reader directly. He contrasts the man of reason with the man of passion, the whore and the innocent, the Unionist and the Nationalist.

And he offers a vivid, exotic mise-en-scène as well, setting the rocky shores of the Donegal seacoast against the verdant inland valleys.

The style combines idyllic descriptions of the Ulster landscapes with clever, telling dialogue. Young Peter Quinn quotes poetry, not because he is a pedant, but because the mood or the circumstance stirs a memory of Yeats or Shelley or Higgins. There is generous imagery in the Yeatsian vision of "red rose, proud rose, sad rose"; symbolic significance in the chaste lily, the passionate rose, and the fallen buds; and metaphoric richness in "blocks of grey houses, silent, with half drawn blinds," the Protestant houses with "a solemn fur-capped Calvinistic appearance." There is humor, too, but it comes in occasional quips of understatement and in the comic relief of one of Mandy's folktales or the bawdy verse of a Gaelic song, rather than the broad ribald humor of the later fiction. The writer succeeds in varying character, scene, and tone.

John Boyd, writing of Kiely in *The Arts in Ulster* (1951), claimed that the novelist had a toughness and a sentimentality not found in any other Ulster writer and that he had a greater awareness of the political and social scene than any other Irish writer. That is perhaps why *Land without Stars* rings true. In his first long fiction, the young novelist from Tyrone writes a convincing narrative that speaks to the significant issues on the Northern Irish scene, creates idealists who are willing to suffer for their convictions, and offers a brutal psychological conflict that strikes directly at the heart. In *Land without Stars* he sets a high mark for the fiction that is to follow.

With *Poor Scholar,* his study of the life of William
Carleton still fresh in mind, Benedict Kiely began
In a Harbour Green. Carleton's influence is unmistakable,
but it is perhaps most obvious in Kiely's sympathetic
portrait of Pat Rafferty, the clever, robust country
hero given to reading and meditation, and in his
river-worshipping father's comparison of his neighbors
to Carleton's Paddy-Go-Easy. But the types, the expres-
sions, and aspects of the countryside bear more than
occasional resemblances to those in Carleton's nineteenth-
century fiction for reasons more justifiable than the
immediacy of *Poor Scholar.* The novelists hail from
neighboring Tyrone valleys, from towns not twenty
miles distant from one another, and the passing of two
or three generations has not eroded the unique character
of the people or the serene beauty of the landscape.
Carleton Country becomes Kiely Country, and Kiely
lays proper claim to it in this 1949 novel.

Land without Stars contributes, in its way, to the success
of the second novel, too. It suggests familiar names,
like Keenan, Kane, and Slevin—and Slevin is, even
in the later novel, "the Republican who will never do
anything but get himself into jail." There are other
common Omagh names, such as Campbell and Mac-
Gowan and Nixon. The setting for *In a Harbour Green*
is remarkably similar to the Ballyclogher area of *Land
without Stars;* it has the ubiquitous rivers and bridges,
courthouse, barracks, lunatic asylum, county hospital,
Catholic church with the imitation Gothic spires,
Devlin Street, and the numerous shops. Ballyclogher
is mentioned as a hamlet four miles down the road from
"the town." The central action begins a year earlier
than the action in *Land,* in the autumn of 1938, and,

apart from the epilogue, it concludes in the spring of 1939.

Events of *In a Harbour Green* bear directly on the author's life in Omagh. The novel opens on a school photograph of fifty-nine boys posed across four neat rows, an actual photograph, with the caption "Christian Brothers School, Boys Choir, Omagh, 1930." Lanty and Gerry Cassidy, Celsus MacCrea, Joe Gilroy, and Benedict Kiely's other boyhood companions are stretched across the face of the photo, and Kiely himself stands fifth from the left in the top row. The author tells of a childhood experience, diving for a shiny sword near the bridge in the Camowen River with Martin McGowan of Omagh, and in the novel Chris Collins and Dinny Campbell fish Bernard Fiddis's sword from under the same bridge. The houses along the Killyclogher Burn in Omagh figure prominently in the story, the Gortin Road is only thinly disguised as the Gortland Road, and the panorama of the nameless riverine town seventy miles from Belfast is described in telling detail.

If the second novel is influenced by the work of Carleton and *Land without Stars* and incidents drawn fron the author's life in and around Omagh, those influences add to the sensitivity and the credibility of the story. Kiely offers a more comprehensive view of life in the Northern Irish town and a socioeconomic cross section of a community that is already twice divided by religion and politics. There are Unionists and Nationalists, Protestants and Catholics, but more importantly, there are castes—the professionals, the merchants and trades-men, and the unfortunate poor who abide always.

Bernard Fiddis is a forty-year-old solicitor who supports the local arts festival and enjoys books, music, whisky, and women. In politics Fiddis describes himself "a moderate Nationalist," though his nationalism is perhaps best illustrated by his empty campaign oratory. He has wealth, position, and imagination, and can escape the ennui of the small town by driving to Belfast, traveling abroad on holiday, spending the evening at Alice Graham's hotel, or penning dark thoughts into his diary. The solicitor is admired and despised by the townspeople who publicly laud his virtues and privately whisper of his promiscuities.

The County Council Secretary tells Mr. Rafferty that nothing can be done about the flooding that threatens the countryside. "We must retrench," he says in his placating tone. To the suggestion that "The Plough and the Stars" be produced as the annual drama, the Monsignor says of O'Casey, "If he wrote the thirty days prayer, it would be a sin to say it." The priest is a narrow-minded censor of literature, football matches, and politics. Jack MacGowan, the bachelor schoolteacher, is a do-nothing idealist who delights in dramatics and lives for the day that he will discover a real talent in the parish hall. And Fiddis sums up the professionals with this entry in his diary: "The politicians and the play-actors and the priests of this town are each in their own ways and in their own degrees irresistibly comic."

Old Campbell represents the *nouveau riche,* the entrepreneur whose gamble on the horseless wagon paid dividends, and his sister Aggie cautiously avoids the town's lower orders to preserve the family's tenuous social position. Tom Nixon, the "respectable" grocer and publican, is one of the parasitic merchants who trades on the ignorance of the poor and raises his own stature by playing practical jokes on drunks and simpletons.

The flourishing market town has its share of poor and downtrodden as well. The Collinses, "though excellent in their own place," belong to Barrack Lane; according to Aunt Aggie, they are descended from a long line of undistinguished British army privates and washerwomen. For Bear Mullan and Joe Keenan, buried in the backstreets of Silver Lane and Crawford's Alley, there are no prospects. Keenan, a talented artist and musician, admits hopelessly, "if you're from the alley, you're damned. You can become a message boy. You can join the bloody army. That's the height of it." Mullan and Keenan rebel; only Brass MacManus seems resigned to his life of poverty.

There are two remaining types—the farmers who live beyond the glare of the gaslamps and the foreigners with business interests in the town. In this novel the Raffertys are the independent Northern farmers who preserve the ancient traditions and have a proper sense of community and sense of justice. They are indigenous to the Ulster landscape as the townspeople are not. Kiely contrasts the honesty and loyalty of the country people with the hypocrisy and self-interest of the townspeople, as he contrasts the beauty of life in nature with the claustrophobic and squalid atmosphere of the town.

Alice Graham, "a foreigner from some backstreet in some unknown city," is a middle-aged Scots divorcee who has, according to rumor, already shed three husbands and marked Bernard Fiddis as next in succession. She reads American magazines, attends fashion shows in Belfast, drinks too much, paints too much, and operates a thriving hotel. But Alice of Caledonia has no business in this town. Pat Rafferty compares her to "a gipsie feeling the want of her own people like a pain in the bowels, for in the town she was an exile, and Bernard Fiddis, in spite of his travels, had his roots here, deep under the houses watered by the river twisted in the earth. . . ." Fiddis will never marry her, and in the end, she will shout obscenities at the crowd from a hotel window while the world passes her by.

Kiely may have marked the dramatic disparities that divide the class-conscious Northern town, but he allows the characters to speak for themselves and leaves the reader to make his own judgments about them. Bernard Fiddis, the Monsignor, and MacGowan, Old Campbell and Tom Nixon, Mullan, Keenan and Mac-Manus, the Raffertys and Alice Graham are the actors in a tragedy that is reenacted in country towns the world over.

There is no central character in the novel unless it be May Campbell, twenty-year-old daughter of the garage proprietor. Like Aunt Aggie, May wants more than the town has to offer, all that a marriage to Bernard Fiddis will guarantee. Ironically, May befriends Alice Graham and profits sufficiently from Alice's counsel to snare Fiddis. She is calculating, willing to gamble Pat Rafferty's love, the family's reputation, and Alice Graham's friendship for her own vainglorious ends. May despises her sister Dympna's low tastes, yet she engages in risqué asides and seduces both Fiddis and young Rafferty. And the author reflects "Fiddis was himself again, felt as he had felt months ago before memories of her face, her tall, strong young body, her hair falling over her shoulders, had commenced following him about as a beautiful evil spirit might follow a doomed man." May is compared first to the Biblical Susannah, innocently tempting the elders; later to the treacherous Delilah. She is insensitive to her aunt's death and passive toward her heartsick father. When May confides to Pat Rafferty that she is not the sort to sacrifice herself for others, he begins, for the first time, to understand the poet's line about the heartlessness of beauty. May Cambell manipulates those about her, and in the end, she succeeds in using Rafferty's child to bait Fiddis into marriage.

The controlling motif is a poem by Robert Wever from which Kiely takes his title: "In a harbour grene aslepe whereas I lay,/ The byrdes sang swete in the middes of the day,/ I dreaméd fast of mirth and play:/ In youth is pleasure, in youth is pleasure." Old John Maxwell, who murdered his wife and was acquitted by the jury, was always a bit odd, not the ordinary dull murderer. There were those haunting memories of youth's pleasures, the honeymoon train to Bundoran, and the first happy years of marriage. Then Maxwell's wife was transformed into a cruel woman with a wicked tongue, and when one day she tempted him to hang her with a rope, he could not resist the temptation. Even if the jury understands Maxwell and acquits him, the spring floods bring God's judgment on him.

Young Rafferty sees in Maxwell's plight more than a dim parallel to his own relationship with May Campbell. He finds himself defending Maxwell against the world that had judged him and against the delusion of beauty that had caused his death. He leaves never to return, the first from the town to die in Hitler's War.

The small town of *In a Harbour Green* is corrupt, hapless, and desperate. The county councilman, the priest, and the schoolmaster are powerless to effect change, for the ills bred into the bankers, shopkeepers, clerks, and laborers have also tainted them. Though the novel is not as scathing as Brinsley MacNamara's satire on that harsh and ugly town of the squinting windows, both towns suffer the same curious social malignancies. But in Kiely there is always a measure of hope in despair— hope in the child born of Pat Rafferty and May Campbell who will be reared by the solicitor, and hope in the future of Jim Collins and Dympna Campbell, and hope in youthful adventurers scouting their imaginary world. And Fiddis will hang the school photograph above his desk in the sitting room, not because he is a masochist, but because he believes a good man can never die, that a good man must be remembered always.

The author is a romantic with an uncommon respect for the *pishrogues*. Pat Rafferty keeps a living trout in the well for good luck, and the mourners at Aunt Aggie's funeral greet one another with "Blessed are the dead that the rain rains on," leaving Jim Collins to complete the adage, "Blessed is the bride that the sun shines on." There is, too, a favorite ghost who haunts a local mansion with his buck goat. And Kiely uses the Gaeltacht setting to find the common denominator of Irish character, the noble savagery of the Western World, and he uses the *féis* to gather the hosts for crises of the soul. He is fond of songs and poems out of the past and introduces them with a generous spontaneity throughout. In "The American Movement and Saroyan" in the *Irish Ecclesiastical Record* two years earlier, he reiterated Saroyan's counsel: "Pay no attention to the speechmaker. Know the politician for a crook. String along with the poet." At times the novel depends on the poem for wit and wisdom. Kiely believes that, while the old ways may not have always been the best, the memory of them is heartwarming. "In youth is pleasure, in youth is pleasure," he sings with the poet.

Kiely's handling of the Wever poem as a major motif is artful, as is his manipulation of the passages from the dark murder story by Gorki. The symbolism suggested by the snow-covered tower, "the sins of the century covered in spotless snow," and the phallic sword that Bernard Fiddis would "plant in some newly-discovered land" are effective, too. But the writer is at his best when his imagination conjures up the marvelous climax that overrides the narrow-minded Monsignor's objection to O'Casey. Kiely stages a torchlight parade and a political meeting, complete with fiery speeches and songs of rebellion, while he plays a surrealistic parody of the scene on the next street. O'Casey would have been proud. Pat Rafferty's confession is made against the background of the rally, and as the young man agonizes, enumerating each sin, the crowd outside roars approval at Fiddis's vacant platitudes. There are character contrasts—Fiddis and Rafferty, May and Dympna, Alice Graham and Aunt Aggie; there are contrasts in setting—the wilds of Donegal and the streets of the Tyrone town and the sprawl of Belfast. There are also frequent references to the American dream—to Eddie

Cantor breaking the monotony of small town life, to the miracle of the TVA river scheme, and to a confident Yankee priest who promises the Allies' support. And there are the occasional bursts of poetic description that color the landscape and add a fourth dimension to Kiely's fiction.

In a Harbour Green offers a realistic picture of the Irish country town with its hypocrisy and small-mindedness, but it is a picture balanced by the promises of the dreams and ambitions of the young. It is sensitive, imaginative, and well written. In Ireland it was banned. In London it was chosen as a selection of the Catholic Book Club.

By mid-century Benedict Kiely had rounded out a decade of living in Dublin. He was by then an established journalist and a recognized writer of fiction—Dublin reporter and Northern novelist. Having his home away from home in Ireland's City, he came to realize that his novels would have to portray life in that city if he wanted them to be taken seriously in the post-Joycean era.

Until *Call for a Miracle* the city that played an important part in his life played an inconsequential part in his fiction. Peter Quinn quit Ballyclogher for Dublin because it offered an escape from the monotony of country life and the promise of a career in journalism, but in *Land without Stars* Dublin was merely suggested now and again through Dowdall's reveries or Peter's imaginings. Only in the last few paragraphs does the reader find Peter caught up in the masses swarming along Talbot and O'Connell Streets. In the second novel, *In a Harbour Green,* Bernard Fiddis, Alice Graham, and May Campbell hie off to Belfast, seventy miles to the east, when the cultural claustrophobia overwhelms them; Dublin has no part in their lives and no part in the novel. But *Call for a Miracle* is the story of Brian Flood, a sub-editor and leader writer for a Dublin daily, and it is a story of three women who have come to the city to give meaning to their lives, and it is the author's first novel about Dublin itself.

Brian narrates the grim account of Mary Fergus's suicide. In the restaurant on O'Connell Street, he is struck by the thought that the curious story that began in the General Post Office some yards away ended in the Liffey not many more yards in the opposite direction. In the winter of '41 Horatio Nelson, Joyce's "onehandled adulterer," still smugly surveyed the throngs with his one good eye, and Cuchulainn was writhing in agony inside the G.P.O. The country, recently risen from its pangs, was divided on the war.

Call for a Miracle is set in Brian Flood's Dublin. For him the city begins just north of O'Connell Street Bridge and moves southward to Westmoreland, Grafton, Nassau, and Dawson Streets, and to Stephen's Green and Merrion Square, frequently intersecting the familiar Dublin of *Portrait, Ulysses,* and *Finnegans Wake:*

> He (Brian) walked with blind energy, checking himself under the gesturing arm of Henry Grattan's statue while a line of lighted buses turned the corner going between Trinity College and Oliver Goldsmith and Edmund Burke and Tom Moore and a public latrine and Henry Grattan and the Bank of Ireland that had once housed a parliament and heard Grattan's voice.

A generation earlier Leopold Bloom "crossed under Tommy Moore's roguish finger at the meeting of the waters" and passed Trinity's surly front and Grattan's parliament in making his rounds. But this novel ranges beyond the City Centre, and beyond North and South Circular Roads, and takes in more of Joyce's microcosm —Howth, the Pigeon House, the Bull Wall, Killiney, Dalkey, Dollymount Strand, and Phoenix Park. They are all there.

Call for a Miracle seems to lend weight to Brother Juniper's theory that people crossing bridges—O'Connell Street or San Luis Rey—are inextricably bound to one another by something beyond the circumstances of the crossing, that accidents are, in fact, providentially designed. According to the laws of probability, the meetings of Brian Flood, Christine, Mary Fergus, and Philomena Kane seem too pat, too coincidental, but in an unbewildering city like Dublin such meetings do occur. Kiely's novel is a psychological study of Brian Flood, who begins the story, an analysis of the mysterious Mary Fergus, his "Woman in Black," and his study of loneliness and the effects of loneliness on the modern psyche.

The fat and fortyish newspaper editor has, after two years of marriage, separated from his wife, the one woman in the world he cannot get along with, and his small daughter knows him only as Mr. Jones, a monthly visitor who calls when her mother is off on an errand. Flood may be strong enough to endure the physical separation, but he reflects time and again how "a man should never be without a daughter." He longs for female companionship and a daughter's attentions and the congenial society of Dublin's pubs. Brian may not fear loneliness, but neither does he prefer it. He is, in effect, the fool of Padraic Pearse's poem, "A fool that hath loved his folly," "A fool that is unrepentant and that soon at the end of all/Shall laugh in his lonely heart," and though he calls for a miracle with the poet, he realizes full well that he is a skeptic, that he can do nothing to bring it about. In the end he confesses that he is "utterly alone."

Of the women in the novel Brian says, "The names were symbols standing for qualities peculiar to each of the three women." Mary and Christine and Philomena. Mary, surely a Magdelene, had abandoned a dissolute life of prostitution and blackmail because she had finally discovered love beside a kind of wooden rack. Christine, on the verge of accepting an illicit romance with Brian, found that she could not overstep the moral impediments conscience imposed. Philomena is the warm, sensitive, generous Tyrone lass. Brian dismisses surnames as superfluous, though they often suggest another dimension of personality. Mary was, after all, the daughter of Fergus, and Fergus, the Ulster king of the *Táin*, was "the manly son of a stallion." Mary's father was, in his wife's eyes, a man "who once walked haloed in fields of light," though he came to be a perverted tyrant, brutalizing his wife and children and leaving Mary a psychologically scarred young woman. Throughout the story Christine's surname and the name of the town that she and Brian hail from are well-guarded secrets; Christine is described in detail as to manner and form, but Brian steadfastly refuses to divulge more than that "telling" first name. And Philomena bears the surname of Jinny Kane, the Omagh lass of ill fame in *Land without Stars,* and the name of the Rafferty's neighbors who would not vacate their cottage, even in the face of the floods. In the Kiely novel Kane has come to suggest poverty and ignorance, honesty and kindness.

Of the three women in *Call for a Miracle* Mary Fergus is the most intriguing and the most tragic. In Freudian fashion the reader begins to piece her life together from her admissions to Philomena about her father's perversity and her blackmailing the skittish adulterer, from Philomena's witnessing her shoplifting the rings, from the detective's confidences to Brian, and from Brian's reflections on the agony of Mary's Circean power to "transform men into swine." The Woman in Black forsakes those who do not matter—the photographer who looks like a crook, the prosperous businessman, and the quiet academic—and attempts to put her life in order. Mary's happiness is, however, short lived, for a Magdelene cannot hope to outrun her reputation in an unbewildering city of a few bridges. The Circean Woman in Black, allotted but a few brief moments of joy in this life, had exhausted them. Brian thinks, "Perhaps Mary is particularly unfortunate, escaping from the chamber of horror of her childhood and girlhood to find her womanhood locked into another chamber of sorrow and suffering." Mary had been damned from the outset.

When Christine stepped into Brian's life after an absence of twenty years, she revived memories of a wasted youth in a country town. The middle years had come on slowly; she was still stately and blond. She welcomed Brian's boyish attentions, the romance of the excursion to Drogheda, and the walk through Ledwidge's lush Meath countryside. Even if they were "two decrepit sentimentalists," as she put it, they had rediscovered love amidst those "hedges drowned in green grass seas." Christine would surely have gone with Brian on that tryst to the lonely cottage in Kerry, but for Father Peter. The priest-fearing, hell-fearing beauty retires to her country town to live out her years dusting the furnishings, rattling her beads, and wondering what might have been.

By contrast to those of Mary and Christine, Philomena Kane's problems are trivial. She is Kiely's Northern *cailín* come to Dublin to better her lot and meet the right man. If Philomena lacks the formal education, she is blessed with uncommon good sense and the virtues necessary to survive the rigors of urban life. She can distinguish between the romance and the reality, though she has an enormous capacity to sympathize. The reader realizes from the start that Philomena's loneliness is but a temporary setback, that she is Mary Fergus's strength and consolation.

Dublin may be unbewildering, but it is a lonely place for the exiles adrift in its streets. But the exiles, in their course, meet every character type and some characters beyond type—domineering mothers, liberated university students, mad journalists, bustling nurses, merry monastics, and solemn pub crawlers. May McCarthy and Evelyn Murray are interfering matrons bent on having their way at all costs. Big Magee is the reporter who thinks in inverted triangles and who mentally composes features worthy of Westbrook Pegler. The journalist looks like a poet and has the sensitivities of a poet, while the Kavanagh-like poet looks every inch a reporter and speaks in witty truisms. There are also nurses, clerics, and serious drinkers who round out the scene.

Then there is Dave Murray, the invalid who releases himself from his spine frame and makes his way to Mary Fergus's flat to prove his love. There is Philomena's "jackeen" tradesman who reads erudite treatises on African wild life. And finally there is Father Peter, the melodeon-playing thaumaturgist, whose humility and simplicity are genuine, though the reader rightfully suspects that his fumbling naiveté and innocent quips are neither fumbling nor innocent. Peter's near blindness seems only to sharpen his psychic vision; he reads men's souls with astounding accuracy. Miracles cannot be produced on demand, of that he seems quite certain, but miracles do happen if there is faith to back them. In fact miracles occur with regularity in this novel, not the Patrician variety—burning bushes, cures by the cartloads, or graveyards dancing jigs—but the more common miracles of laughter, love, understanding, and compassion where there was none before. And Dave Murray's descent from his cross becomes something more than a symbolic sacrifice because it is the ultimate act of love and a reenactment of the most perfect of miracles.

Father Peter appreciates that Brian Flood's marital predicament is insoluble, that Mary Fergus has been victimized from childhood, that Christine's relationship with Brian is impossible, that Dave Murray may be forced to live out his life on a wooden rack, but he offers no easy answers and he performs no feats: "It is a splendid thing to be with the saints in glory/But to meet the saints on earth is a hell of another story," he quips. At times Father Peter is the epitome of Irish monkdom, counseling Christine in sage religious cliches—"the good can afford to be lonely"; "the strong can afford to be lonely"; "Never less alone than when alone." Christine would have to return to that town that had a way of withering things and people, and Mary and Dave would choose death to loneliness, and Brian would remember guiltily the child playing wisely in a lonely garden, and he would realize what he had lost.

Call for a Miracle draws title and meaning from Padraic Pearse's poem. Having squandered his youth and attempted the impossible, the fool of the poem throws himself on the mercy of God, for God's mercy is all that matters in the last analysis. Kiely again elects to echo the wisdom of the poets, offering snatches of Campbell's "As I Came Over the Grey, Grey Hills," Pearse's translation of "Tara Is Grass," and several ballads set to music. And Big Magee has to be drawn larger than life, not simply because of his stature, but because he has the heart of a poet. But in *Call for a Miracle* it is Kiely who comes off best, for he provides through a rich lyrical prose style, marvelous passages describing gulls in flight and escapes to the mountainy quietude. The novelist effectively manipulates setting to complement a narrative of simultaneous action.

Miracles are neither bargains nor outright gifts; they come with strings. And when Brian finally looks for God to pull the strings and put him on the bus that will take him back to his wife and daughter, that miracle doesn't happen. He reflects with the author that the only miracles that seem to matter in these times are those that destroy human life and blast whole cities out of existence. But Father Peter says it best:

People that live in the world and manage to make a success of it would make you tired telling you that every day of the year they gain something, a new piece of knowledge, or maybe they make some money. But for everything they gain they lose something or they may lose twice as much as they gain. That's the law behind everything. Even when you ask something from God you must be prepared to give up something else.

Call for a Miracle is essentially a psychological study of four exiles adrift in Dublin, of their attempts to salvage something of their lives and make peace with God, but it is also a serious novelistic inquiry into certain metaphysical questions. Is there a grand design according to which man serves his time on earth, a divine plan which cannot be thwarted by the human will? Brother Juniper and Brian Flood will travel many a mile and cross many a bridge before they unravel the mystery. It has been suggested that in this novel of conscience Benedict Kiely also touches common ground with Graham Greene, that there are striking similarities in theme and treatment, but Kiely is, in every sense, his own man, and *Call for a Miracle* is an integral part of the Kiely canon. The novel examines the philosophical questions that give direction to the later work, and it anticipates situations and characters that appear later.

Kiely seems to have an intuitive sense of narrative design and technique, a sense that may emanate from an awareness of the *sean sgéal*, what may be loosely termed "the Irish novel tradition." The complexities of his plot, his intricate patterning, and asides in poetry, song, and anecdote, combine to make a well-wrought long story.

What's more, his early novels have the stylistic strengths of the short fiction, of "Blackbird in the Bramble Bough," "The Pilgrims," and "Rich and Rare Were the Gems She Wore."

The Ballyclogher-to-Dublin novels show a discernible movement from village to town to city, but they also chart a discernible maturity in Kiely's technique. *Land without Stars* is more than a "passable" first novel, it is compelling fiction by a first-rate writer. *In a Harbour Green* rivals MacNamara's *Valley of the Squinting Windows* as a realistic portrayal of the narrowness of rural Irish life. And *Call for a Miracle* raises awesome questions that few other Irish Catholic writers have had the courage to ask.

4

Through A Glass Darkly:
Four Novels, 1952–1960

"The road went one way towards the village and the city, and the other way to plunge into dark country." In *Honey Seems Bitter* (1952) Donagh Hartigan, a civil servant suffering from a case of nerves, narrates events stemming from a murder in a small village within commuting distance of Dublin. Recently discharged from a convalescent home, he rents a cabin, packs his library, and sets out for a rest cure in the country. But the investigation of Lily Morgan's murder and his involvement with the villagers leave him little time to reflect on the thoughts of existential writers or to brood about his nervous condition. The gaunt old mill with the sightless windows, the small clusters of houses, and the winding rivers soon give way to a Dublin lounge bar, a crowded racecourse, and a courtroom where death hangs in the air. Even the countryside is a place of dark thoughts and dark deeds.

Honey Seems Bitter is a thriller and a love story and a psychological study all in one. It is for the reader to determine whether the murder mystery or the romantic

triangle or Donagh Hartigan's psychic introspection
should take precedence. Whichever he decides he will
not be disappointed, for Kiely manages to weave the
three strands into a whole cloth with customary novelistic genius.

Is Donagh Hartigan to be pitied or admired? He
experiences anxiety apparently brought on by the attentions of doting mother and sisters. He lacks confidence in his ability to perform in the real world, so he
gravitates to "divining the mystics" and losing himself
in "sententious meditations about the horrors of modern
war." As the murder trial begins, Butler, shocked at
Donagh's perversity, assails him: "You enjoy this,
Harty, you microbe . . . You get a kick out of it. An
intellectual pleasure. Where's your pity? That bastard
in the dock? That girl on the bed?" And, though Donagh
shuns the pressures of appearing at the inquest, he rel-
ishes the notoriety attached to discovering the corpse.

Admittedly Donagh Hartigan is full of dark thoughts.
He tells us, for example, how he reads Kafka's dismal
diaries "with positive pleasure," how he is obsessed
with Gorki studying gorillalike murderers and Graham
Greene suffering dysentery in a Mexican ditch. Confused by the metaphysicians and the mystics, Donagh
concedes in the end that life is opaque, ambiguous, and
irrational. To Mrs. Morgan's "It's little any of us knows
of the wickedness the devil puts into the heart of man,"
he responds, "That's true. That's true." And one imagines that Pascal, Sartre, and Dostoevsky look up from
dusty notebooks to nod assent.

There are four other writers whose works give direction to Donagh's ruminations. Eustache Deschamps,

the fourteenth-century Provencal poet and author of *Le Miroir de Mariage,* provides the recurring lines, "J ay dur sein et hault assis./ Sui-je, sui-je, sui-je belle?" to mark Emily Rayel's progress. Marcus Aurelius's "Sixth Meditation," suggests the title: "To the jaundiced honey tastes bitter, and to those bitten by mad dogs water causes fear; and to little children the ball is a fine thing." Donagh might have added "To the cynic there is only ruin and desolation." But Marcus the Meditator had been betrayed by his wife, Faustina, as Proteus, of Shakespeare's *Two Gentlemen,* had betrayed friendships, as indeed Donagh had decided to betray George Butler, who he thought was his friend. The repeated references to Deschamps, Aurelius, and Shakespeare serve to interrelate the familiar theme of betrayal in French, Latin, and English classics and heighten Hartigan's awareness of the foulness of his deed.

Appropriately the fourth reference is to an ancient Gaelic folktale about the resolution of a feud. The story offers no explanations, no morals, though it implies that a man may live a whole life of dream in a moment of stabbing someone and withdrawing the blade. Donagh can end his dream by a single act of conscience. "To end the dream might save Jim Walsh and restore Lily Morgan to life, but those things, as desirable as they might be, would for me be no recompense for the loss of Emily Rayel." In the end, with Butler and Walsh dead and Emily forever lost, he wonders if the skian lies hidden under the eaves of his cabin.

On the surface George Butler is Donagh Hartigan's antithesis—self-assured extrovert, ad man and film and drama reviewer, cosmopolite whose bravado is legend-

ary. When Butler befriends "Harty" and introduces him
to the villagers, to Emily Rayel, and to the habitués of
Pyramid Lounge in Dublin, Donagh is understandably
indebted, though still he harbors a resentment toward
Butler for his popularity. "It appeared to be an honour
to be one of those who saluted that swaggering has-
tening man; and listening for the greetings, watching
hands raising the tumblers as if for wassail, I was proud
of him. Being in his royal company gave me status,"
says Donagh. But it was George Butler who lured him
to Lily Morgan's bed, Butler who strangled the girl, and
Butler who stood by and allowed Jim Walsh to be hanged
in his stead. Hearing the contempt in his voice, Donagh reflects, "If it did anything to me, it made me
ferociously glad, certain that he was no longer my friend,
that he never could have been my friend." And what of
little Emily who dances to Deschamps' music? "Tell
me, am I, am I, am I beautiful?" Emily of the *Roman* is
absorbed in Butler's conversations and attracted by his
manner, yet she fears him. When George defends her
honor at the racetrack pub, she is repulsed by his actions: "I hate scenes. I hate violence. I hate strong men,"
she tells an acquaintance. But why does Emily confide
in Donagh Hartigan? Why does she agree to the rendez-
vous? And, finally, why does she willingly sacrifice her
virginity to him? Is it that Donagh is weaker and less
threatening, that Emily, with her childlike lisp and her
womanly frigidity, shares his anxieties and insecurities?
He suspects from the start that she is calculating and he
wonders at her preference for him over Butler.

After Butler's death Donagh Hartigan asks himself,

"Should I have known all the time who was the murderer of Lily Morgan?" It is the question that measures the
novel's success as a mystery story and the question that
the reader must ultimately put to himself. Had George
Butler's behavior over those months offered a clue to
his guilt or his motives? In retrospect it would appear
that it had. As the trial draws nearer and Emily Rayel
is more distant, Butler becomes more irascible. He is
on a continuous drunk, he invites physical confronta-
tions, and, on one occasion, he buttonholes Donagh
with a bellicose fierceness. Finally Hartigan tells us,
"After months of silence he was talking, talking, talking, as even the prince of devils must surely talk confid-
ingly to some other black angel. (Butler shouts,) 'Then
you came along with your nerves. Jesus. Nerves. How
little you knew about it. What do you think my nerves
were like all the time. Jitters. Jitters. I could hardly keep
myself from driving the car under a bus or something,
or into the river off the city quays.' "

Donagh knows a good deal more than he reveals—he
had been acquainted with Lily Morgan, he knew Jim
Walsh's whereabouts on the night of the murder, and
he sensed that there was more to Butler's silence than
he himself wanted to know. It is only the threat of Emily's leaving for England with Butler that lands Donagh
in the police station to offer evidence. But Butler fulfills
his own prophesy by driving his car into the river off the
city quays, and Donagh's love for Emily Rayel dies
with him.

"There was nothing reliable in the world, nothing
steady, nothing competently known," Donagh con-

cludes. George Butler was not really a friend, Jim Walsh had killed no one, Emily's love was selfish. Irrelevant people with their irrelevant statements convict an innocent man, and Mrs. Morgan, a perjurer, utters the parting truism on human corruptibility. The neurotic Donagh gains confidence while the confident George Butler becomes a neurotic. And it is, in Donagh's imaginings, Lily who lies on the ancient fort in the sunny whin-sheltered corner and Emily who lies on the bed screaming before strangling hands. "There was nothing reliable in the world, nothing steady, nothing competently known."

Is Donagh Hartigan to be pitied or admired? He voluntarily seeks entry to the psychopathic world of Kafka, Sartre, and Dostoevsky; he treacherously betrays a man he believes to be his friend; and he takes perverse delight in witnessing or imagining human misery. But Hartigan is, for all that, a fascinating character, one of the most fascinating in the Kiely gallery. The author has drawn him without compassion, a weak, selfish, bookish little man who broods with the intensity of Dostoevsky's diarist. If there is any pity it must be reserved for Butler, who, in a reckless moment, kills Lily Morgan, suffers agonizingly through the trial and its aftermath, and realizes at last that he has lost Emily, too.

There are in *Honey Seems Bitter* the delightful stylistic passages that have come to be expected of Kiely. In one passage Donagh's passions erupt amid the lush tropical foliage of the Botanical Gardens, an eroticism fired by exoticism of place and name, and, in a second, the mystical forces of an ancient fairy fort are unleashed.

Halfway up, I felt, a satyr or a goat itself or an ancient crooked shepherd would carry on the wondertale rhythm, would show us a clear spring where every drinker of the pure cold water could find power to love and live forever.

Donagh is again driven to goat madness, infected by the powers of a mythical presence. But over and against these fantaisies, there are the sordid details, nauseating sights and smells and the vivid memory of "a slattern of a woman chewing the bacon rinds of a late breakfast" and pouring the drinks.

Through his first three novels one recognizes Kiely's preoccupation with loneliness and intellectual barrenness and his unmistakable progression toward existentialism. *Honey Seems Bitter* is the culmination of that effort. Donagh Hartigan, as intriguing and convincing a character as he is, represents the dark side of humankind and voices the hidden fears of all humanity. He is obsessed with sin and guilt and the threat of instant annihilation; he is acutely aware of both sexual and spiritual natures. Hartigan does not resist moral choices; he says No, and thereby posits his existence. Kiely's is a godly brand of existentialism and *Honey Seems Bitter* one of the finest modern Irish novels in the mode. What an irony that, though the novel was published by Dutton in New York (1952), by Methuen in London (1954), and republished, under the title *The Evil Men Do,* by Dell in New York (1954), the Board of Censorship of Publications banned it in Ireland.

If Kiely admits to sometimes hearing the muted voice of the Gaelic story-teller accompanied by the rush of wind in the bushes and the thundering of waves on the shore, surely those phantasms affect *The Cards of the Gambler*

(1953) more than any other of his works. The folktale rendered by the tweedy *seanachie* in the thatched Gaeltacht cottage provides a frame, indeed more than a frame for this fifth novel. The ancient narrative that is reproduced with all of its· nuances through prologue, epilogue, and seven interludes, charts the progress of the modern novel and furnishes characters, incidents, and devices. The tale is ready-made.

The fuller reading of *Cards* depends upon an understanding of Celtic mythology and symbolism, as well as an understanding of the pagan-Christian syncretism that fails to come to grips with essential questions. What Kiely does in *Cards* is to offer universalized conceptualizations of God and Death and hell, and inquire further into the elusive distinction between "what is" and "what appears to be." "Some dreams are true," Death tells the doctor-gambler. But can we posit reality and distinguish between good and evil? The gambler decides that he should have asked God, as his third request, to tell him the how and the why of things, "for in heaven one learns a lot. The hell of hell is that the soul endures so much and finds out nothing." *Cards* is, then, a philosophical allegory that probes beyond the existential issues raised in the earlier novels.

The ninety-year-old *seanachie* relates the tale his forefathers heard from a traveling man in the eighteenth century, and the novelist, in his introduction, cautions his audience, "As for me, I heard it from the man you're watching, and you, if you wait, will hear it from me. When I come to tell it, I will also add, subtract, divide, and multiply." It is, however, the old man's story that must first be told. The Gaelic narrative, recast as the author promised, is set against the background of Dublin lounge bars, a swank country club, and suburban estates, but the consciousness of that eighteenth-century Gaelic life is felt throughout, in memories of swaggering chieftains, dying honor, and "a soft ancestral language" whispered in poetry and ballads. There is, too, a harkening back beyond that century and beyond the Celtic twilight to the dimmer, more distant past, as Kiely manages to blend simplicity of design and psychological intensity to effect fiction that succeds as *sean-sgéal* and modern novel.

In this universe God is the thirteenth man, a handsome young cleric with golden hair who seeks the solitude of the mountainy furze and "a mound of grey stones carried to the summit in some lost age to build a burial place, or a temple to the sun and the wind." The latter-day Aengus scatters the sunlight while twelve dark-visaged dervishes dance a satellite ritual of life, of death. God is aloof, a sophisticated polyglot, a gourmet, a loner, and something of chancer himself: "Creation was a game and God putting a man and a woman in a testing garden was the first gambler, and all gamblers must be close to the heart of God."

Death is God's contact man, his facilitator. "I do the overtaking," he says. He prides himself on a near-perfect record, comically recalling his last slip as an eighteenth-century mishap at an apple tree. He confesses a weakness for reading *Crime and Punishment,* and he preserves news clippings and bone trophies in his black briefcase. Death comes unexpectedly and comes variously disguised as a spitting greybeard, a vicious soldier, a Spaniard in a duffle coat, a Frenchman with two profiles, a devil-possessed giant, and as darkness in a room. Feared and friendless, he admits to the gambler that in the final moment of life there are no calm heroes or cool martyrs. And the conflict in the novel is summed up in the wisdom of "a man must break his promise, Death never can."

In *Cards* the gambler-doctor matches wits with Death time and again, and though he snatches the Spanish nobleman from Death's clutches, he loses the man's young wife, as he loses his children's puppy and the woman he loves and his only son. He reflects that life begins to change when man seriously contemplates God and Death. In the words of the poet, "He knows Death to the bone/Man has created Death."

The novel opens in a golf clubhouse where seven exhausted gamblers face "a green field where kings and queens and jesters in two different colors, red for blood and black for death, lie on beds of red diamonds, dark trefoil, bleeding hearts, and heads of black spears." In life the doctor had at last reached the abyss of negative perfection, losing all of his wordly goods, down to the overcoat he was wearing. The automobile he once owned runs out of gasoline before he reaches home, his wife and family desert him. Complete deprivation. No remorse. The gambler joins ranks with Brian Flood and Donagh Hartigan, taking a perverse consolation in having plumbed the depths of abject depravity, invited an incestuous relationship, and achieved a sense of utter loneliness.

His postmortem reflections are more than mere afterthoughts, for they question again the nature of God, the significance of damnation, and the purpose of life.

"God is light. God is a bright day," concludes the hypnotist, reviving the age-old notion that the unapproachable divinity brings light into darkness and nothing more. The reality is hell, and "hell," says the doctor, "is oneself." In the Middle Ages the Dantean inferno with its licking flames and red demons was livelier, but then every man in every age dreams his own hell. For the twentieth-century man it is loneliness, isolation, and ennui that mark its parameters, and for the doctor with the eighteenth-century soul it is middle class respectability and suburban hypocrisy that fan the fires. Life is the gamble that God may be approached and hell averted, but life is measured by the single question, "Did they (mankind) gain or did they lose by meeting you?" The balance in his favor, the game is won.

The Cards of the Gambler is replete with symbolism—cabalistic, numerological, mythological, and chromatic. Twelve Oriental apostles dance circular configurations around the immutable God; three, seven, and nine are the recurring numbers; a golden-haired Aengus seeks the comfort of airy heights near an ancient stone circle; and the red and the black of the cards signify always blood and death.

And, of course, the poets—Milton, Dante, and Yeats—will have their say, for the novelist heeds Saroyan and sticks with the poet for wit and wisdom. There are, among many successful techniques, the two anecdotal letters, the "Dialogue Between Two Women," "The Monologue of a Forgiving Wife to a Dark Husband," the three "Awakenings," and the elaborate personification of allegorical figures to set the tone for Kiely's variation on the Gaelic source. It is the folktale, rendered in its entirety through the interludes, that is Kiely's masterstroke in this novel, and *Cards* succeeds because of his skill as a *seanachie* and his talent as writer of modern fiction.

In the spaciousness of the Irish Midlands there stood an eighteenth-century Georgian house that was "renowned for sacred lore and pure unspotted life," not unlike that house of Spenser's. It is the setting for *There Was an Ancient House* (1955). In time, manse and demesne, held by Anglo-Irish gentry, passed from convert Countess to pious celibates by act of religious generosity. Splendid drawing rooms transformed to modest chapels, profane statuary of half-clad Greek divinities displaced by plastic saints, the Big House still dominated the sleepy village adjacent to it and formed, as it were, a temporal link between the ruin of a nearby Norman tower and the paltry architectural evidence of a more recent civilization. And in that ancient house eighteen Irish novices tested their spirituality, their self-discipline; some survived the rigors, others did not. "Sweet little bell/ That is struck in the windy night,/I liefer go to a tryst with thee/Than to a tryst with a foolish woman."

Barragry, a Dublin journalist with a distinct literary flair, recently arrived at the holy house in the Midlands, resolves:

When I get back to the world I'll write a novel about this place: the lake and the trees, the seclusion from everything, even newspapers, the prayer, the charity, the peace, the blues, the noonday devil, the fear for perseverance, the long corridors and high rooms that like myself remember the world, the leper colony with its tattered suits of clothes, the one room where the white, ancient, naked statuary of dead days has, for the sake of decorum, been decently stored away.

A novel set in such a place is simply too fascinating to pass up. And Ben Kiely's experiences in that ancient house, the Jesuit novitiate at Emo Park, Co. Laois, stirred the same resolve. The book begged to be written.

There Was an Ancient House is a novel of colors and contrasts. The chaste whiteness of spirituality clashes with the greyness, brownness, and blackness of MacKenna's Ulster provincial town, and the red and white laughter of curious youth fades and vanishes in the golden sunburst of a monstrance held aloft. MacKenna's final vision is that of a multicolored hospital: "It was," he remembers, "black and white, blue and white, grey and white, blue and red, all the colours of nursing nuns and teaching nuns, of nurses, ward-maids, shouting boys and girls." The Kiely palette has never run richer.

In the novel color is not the only contrast, however, the disparity in religious and secular life is effected by frequent intrusions of physical on spiritual and vice versa. Barragry is particularly troubled at the stilted conversations between religious and laymen, and he is obviously disturbed that he hasn't a bob to give the wretch in the workhouse for a pint. MacKenna's perilous journey to the hospital in Dublin is starkly countered by the rollicking ramble into the Midlands by Beauchamp and Co. And his pious meditations are constantly shattered by lascivious imaginings of Frankie and Delia tumbling in the grass of the Killyclogher woods or his own aborted sexual exploits on the railway embankment. Within the ancient house the lonely world of the spirit and the crowded world of the flesh were simply incompatible.

Jim MacKenna is a young Ulster poet, a Bartlett with a propensity for quoting the poem for the occasion. "Poems, poems, poems, and prayers," he says. Among the procession of rhymers who find their way into the novel are American, English, and Irish poets of distinction, but it is Spenser and the *Faerie Queene* that provide motif, inspiration, and title for the novel. Dame Caelia strides the ancient corridors, candle in hand, posturing herself as Kiely's Mrs. Macbeth. But, when the poet is struck by a spinal disease and removed from ancient house to modern orthopedic hospital, his scruples dissipate with the change of wind. A new kind of poetry is in the offing.

> My name is Barragry and I come from Dublin. I'm one of the better sort of people, even if in the world I did work for a newspaper. I meditate regularly and use the discipline twice a week, perfunctorily, and, odd as it may seem, I was some time since smitten with a vague idea of becoming a priest. I take size sixteen and a half in collars and I abandoned a mistress to the tender mercies of the world.

Journalist, barrister, and one-time literary editor, Barragry is described as "amusingly cynical." Above all he is forthright about asking questions: "Why do we come? Do we know why we come? Do we know what we leave behind?" In fact he realizes that his own motives are suspect; he has deserted a mistress after sending her on "their secret mission to London." Remorse for his part in the "mission" had driven him to the brink of despair, and despair had driven him into the religious life. In that year Barragry had his answers: "Living among the saints taught me a lot, taught me how much of a hound I was." He knew at last what he had come to and what he had left behind.

But what of the others? Why had they come? Mac-Kenna perhaps in search of aesthetic perfection and to be privy to the respected tradition of the house. Petit, the Latin scholar, because asceticism was in his bones. Donnelly, the bishop's nephew, because the sacerdotal life was expected of him. Barnes, the man of affluence, perhaps to satisfy a yearning for more bread and less cake.

Of the other religious, the Magnov, the Master of Novices, is particularly well drawn. Like Father Peter in *Call for a Miracle,* the Magnov has an infallible sense of order and a warm sense of humor. Then there are Brother O'Rhattigan and Brother Matthews: O'Rhattigan has been frightened from his bathing beauty into the religious life by the sight of a rotting corpse, and Matthews, deprived of equine experiences, fabricates derbys for the aged poor. For these and for the legendary Father Willy Doyle the religious life held the happiness that might very well lead to broken doors and cramped quarters.

The memorable characters not of the cloth include Barragry's friend Beauchamp, artist-creator of "The Stinking Pit," a marvelous Dantean fantasy on canvas; Eddy, Beauchamp's randy sidekick, and Barr's delightful free-spirited mistress. Their pub-hopping excursion from Dublin to the Midland villa, an irreverent journey to discover God knows what, is replete with bawdy taunts and inane anecdotes. The triune scouting party staggering its way through the woodland demesne are the refugees from Cooper's *Leatherstocking,* and Beauchamp's avian antics and the girl's sacrilegious dip in the sacred waterhole add a touch of frenzy to the pace. The ribald world of the flesh sends ripples through the ordered world of the spirit and all the while there is a mimetic suggestion that advances the notion of desperation in both worlds.

The Latinisms, the hagiographies, and lists of sacred authors; the "semper" that punctuates each errant utterance; the meditations, examines, and the flagellations help to create the difficult atmosphere of "pure, unspotted life." The Latin phrases capture the prayerful mood, and, carefully read, they provide occasional light humor as well. To balance the mood, though, Kiely introduces numerous witty asides and puts Barragry's "amusing cynicism" to good use: "Being holy is thirsty work," thinks Barr, en route to finding a "watering place."

As noted earlier, *There Was an Ancient House* comes out of the author's personal experiences in the Jesuit novitiate, but it is not so esoteric as to be discounted as a successful novel. On the contrary, Kiely offers here a realistic account of the tenor of novitiate life and a novel that is ostensibly religious in tone, mood and theme. In the process he sketches a collection of sensitive and amusing characters, giving the reader, as it were, the best of both worlds. Behind the scenes the wily novelist slings his heavy brush with reckless abandon and smiles a tight-lipped smile. There is more than meets the eye.

Brian Flood of *Call for a Miracle* is left "utterly alone": "men grow more and more afraid of the face above the hand that pulls the strings," he concludes. In the end of *Honey Seems Bitter* Donagh Hartigan accepts his negative isolation as a fact of life, and the doctor-gambler of *Cards* questions the meaning of the here and the hereafter. Is there the same existential concern with loneliness and despair in this novel? *There Was an Ancient House* offers Kiely's reflections on an earlier period when there was faith or faint doubts, and it offers reminiscences of a youth crowded with pleasant memories: "In the world one never had such good company," he tells us.

Coming as it does, after *Call for a Miracle, Honey Seems Bitter,* and *The Cards of the Gambler,* it is not at all surprising to find that MacKenna and Barragry are both conscience-ridden victims of a spiritual-sexual conflict, and that Pascal and Ignatius exhort them to relinquish their humanity to the higher order. But Barragry asks himself, "Is it good for one to adhere to God merely because destruction is the penalty for nonadherence?" The journalist will say no; he will leave the ancient house for the world. Despite the illusion that divine intercession is at work shaping one's destiny, what is important in the final analysis is that man be afforded the veto. Spenser's "auncient house not far away, renowned throughout the world for sacred lore" becomes "old Spenser's Cave of Despayre; dark, doleful, dreary, like a greedy cave, that still for carrion carcases doth crave." Is the novel so much more positive or is it simply reflective?

There Was an Ancient House, published in part in *Irish Writing,* introduces or further develops many of Kiely's successful techniques, but it represents no radical philosophical departure. In it one sees the color patterns of

"The Pilgrims," the reveries of youth of "Down Then by Derry," and the shadowings of setting and character and the allusions of *Dogs Enjoy the Morning.*

Benedict Kiely's seventh novel, *The Captain with the Whiskers* (1960), comes five years after *There Was an Ancient House* and demonstrates once again his ingenious skill for spinning out several skeins of a complex plot and concocting a kind of verbal wizardy in the process. The vivid landscapes and frequent poetic runs of songs and ballads meld easily with the poetry of Yeats and Stephens and Kavanagh to create an atmosphere that shifts from lovely to wistful to fantastic with the force of the wind or the mood of the poet. An Irish Boer War ballad, several of its verses neatly woven into the narrative texture, gives title to the novel; Ledean Swans wing ominously through the pattern, suggesting always psychic transmigrations; and withal, there is the inimitable touch of the Tyrone novelist whose imagination has run wilder than ever in this, his latest work.

Modern novelists, according to Kiely, are more preoccupied with the psychology of evil, the problem of divine estrangement, and the nature of the mythopoeic act than they are with the normal and the natural. Owen Rodgers repeats Dr. Grierson's conundrum with alarming frequency through the novel, "Is it better to be born and damned than not to be born at all?" The question may unnerve the reader, but it is essential to a grasp of the author's intent.

The Captain with the Whiskers is the study of a psychopathic martinet, his wife and five children, and it is the story of Owen Rodgers, the narrator, who is drawn into the inner sanctum of Bingen House by the mutual fascination that exists between the Captain and himself. "If I have a friend in Bingen," he muses, "it is the captain with the whiskers." Owen discovers that the Captain has an abiding respect for German efficiency and Prussian discipline and no respect for his indolent Irish neighbors or their traditions. By his decree Magheracolton becomes Bingen.

The Captain's encyclopedic knowledge ranges from alchemy to zoology, and the strange love-hate relationship he develops with his family and with young Rodgers stems from an inner darkness, a sadomasochism just below the surface. His cruelty is legend; he brutalizes his wife and children, eventually bringing ruin on their heads. But it is not simply the Captain's perversity that intrigues the young narrator; Owen is also taken with the notion that, even if a sardonic God showed no mercy to the Captain's widow or his orphaned progeny, he himself might impose order on the chaos, if he chose to. But, like Donagh Hartigan he elects to maintain his distance; he takes an intellectual pleasure in witnessing the disintegration of the Chesneys.

The novel is also a study of Bingen House, the house presided over by the baleful serpent and "the captain's ghost darting in and out like a diabolized Ariel." Gone is the Captain who reorganized the world; gone, too, is the mien of prosperity that once graced the land. The patriarchal tyranny that would dominate Bingen from beyond the grave finds no voice. Nature creeps determined from an Ulster mountain, bursts from a swollen river, and lashes from the Atlantic tempests to destroy the Captain's handiwork, to reclaim Macheracolton to itself: "All those white, laughing cataracts had conspired together. God and the Gortin river, and the old gods of rock and water, grass and bush, who, before Bingen had answered to the name Magheracolton, had watched the captain for years, waiting for this ultimate, ludicrous moment."

With the death of the Captain, confusion and mutiny broke out, leading to dissolution and despair. Alfred, the heir apparent, frequented pubs and brothels and was finally imprisoned for molesting a fourteen-year-old neighbor whore. The sallow haunted ascetic, Father Francis, was driven into his clerical role by a mysterious force. The cowardly Edmund, returned from England, dashing, bearded and boastful, softened his skull in an auto collision.

The sins of the father visited on the sons, the Conway Chesney empire crumbles with the ineptitude and dementia of the heirs, and Owen Rodgers denies his fosterage and refuses to arrest the destruction. Meanwhile, a Brannigan seaman, a Firbolg opportunist, stands patiently at the gates with his bid. Jeff Macsorley had never written his Southern novel, *The Book of Bingen* or *The Monster of Magheracolton,* but there is a distinct feeling that Bingen connects to Yoknapatawpha and that the Chesneys and Comptons are at least far-out relations.

Women are born to be damned, says Greta Chesney. Her own mother as a skivvy under house arrest could cope with the reality of the Captain's cruelty but not with his death. Maeve, the wild queen, freed from the Captain's malevolence, emerges wanton and unbridled, and despite Owen's efforts to tame her, she slips the bond and flees Bingen forever. She might find love with Kinnear, Macsorley, Molphy, or Beverley but never with her dead father's protégé. Greta, obsessed by the poison in her veins, shrinks from life like Rappacini's daughter. Owen seduces her and promises to find her a job in the city, but there is no altruism in the promise; he does it rather "to show my captain's power over the life of this hidden female." Greta's suicide, the grotesque details—the priest and dock-laborer piecing her skull together—shock Owen to a fuller awareness of his Judas complex. Mesmerized by the wickedness of Captain Conway Chesney who was damned, he realizes that his own part was perhaps more perverse. He had willed to stand by, a morbid observer of the disintegration and decay at Bingen.

As foils to the Captain's sordidness, Kiely presents the genial and cultivated John Rodgers and the sophisticated Dr. Grierson. Owen's father can forgive Mickey Doran, the wizard on Segully Mountain, for amputating the rate collector's finger or keeping his sister's corpse from the grave to collect on her pension, but not the Captain who has reorganized the topography and rechristened the townland. John Rodgers knew that the Captain's "destruction" had more dire consequences. The venerable Dr. Grierson, a priest whose alcoholism distracts him from his loneliness, cursed the Captain as "devil incarnate."

James Kinnear becomes a barrister and Jeff Macsorley a writer, but Owen rejects medicine to become a successful hotelier. We are given to believe that his marriage to the plump Lucy with the unfailing sense of propriety and an acquaintance with the *Social Directory* had, up to the time of her death, been satisfactory. He had, of course, loved Maeve, not Lucy, but now, in retrospect, he could not decide how much of Maeve and the Captain and Bingen was dream and how much was reality. The normal son of a normal man concludes, "Even now I doubt if the Captain was a monster."

Owen knew it was better to be born and damned than never to be born at all, as Stephen Dedalus knew that he must err, "even a great mistake, a lifelong mistake as long as eternity, too." And who made Owen Rodgers? God made him, and a priest, a scholar, a drunkard, a soldier, a monster, a kindly musical man, a wizard from wet mountains: God the father in seven mystical shapes. There is loveliness, wistfulness and fantasy in *The Captain with the Whiskers*, but there is, too, acceptance rather than despair.

Though Gortin and Killeter suggest an Omagh setting, Kiely has blended his Strule Valley landscape with that of Derry and the Foyle and the Diamond and "the Winged Victory" and the great Guildhall inside the city walls, and with the landscape of Inishowen Head, where sheep dog trials have been known to happen and where there is a curious old house resembling Bingen. With this novel the reader cannot help but sing the strange refrain of the Boer War ballad or help but laugh good-naturedly at the *pishrogues* or help but feel a bit queasy at the thought of Kate Carr's satyr juice. There is the chance that he will remember Hughie and Lizzie Heron or the hairy Macillions or the jockey Fee, but there is no chance whatever that he will forget the Captain with the whiskers.

5

Mad Dogs and Irishmen:
Dogs Enjoy the Morning

Benedict Kiely's *Dogs Enjoy the Morning* was published eight years after *The Captain with the Whiskers*. It appears different from the earlier Kiely novels—a departure in style, in mood, in technique. In this eighth novel the author goes beyond revealing the myriad of contradictions that trouble the Irish soul; here he throws brickbats at its puritanical facade and its petty foibles. Kiely qualifies the satire with generous doses of wit and humor interspersed to soften the indignation. John Wilson Foster suggests, in a 1969 *Dublin Magazine* exegesis, that the novel may be "in the nature of a fictional summing-up" because all of the Kiely motifs and themes are represented, though it is perhaps more reasonable to assume that the author deliberately reintroduces the motifs and themes as an undergirding for a *magnum opus*. *Dogs Enjoy the Morning* is different from the earlier novels; it is more complicated fiction in a more complex style, a style that effectively integrates the author's narrative strengths. It is aesthetically more developed than the earlier long fiction, and it gives the reader a Benedict Kiely who is now more angry and more confident than the novelist who left Ireland for America four years before. As a major novel by a major writer, *Dogs Enjoy the Morning* must be counted among the important works in contemporary Irish fiction.

The novel is not, however, a complete departure; it is the same Kiely who ranged far and wide creating an undisciplined fantasy that says at every turning: "There is more to life than meets the eye." It is the same Kiely who teases the reader into asking why it is that dogs enjoy the morning. Is it that the morning air is clearer, that the scent is fresher then, that morning activity is brisker, or does the secret lie in simply being a dog or being doglike, in being unfettered to sense all life in nature? It is the same Kiely who weaves myth, folklore, religion, rebellion, exile, and romance into a sensible fictional pattern; who contrasts pagan and Christian, ascetic and sexual, rural and urban, youth and old age; who develops a host of convincing characters from that strange half-light of experience and imagination. *Dogs Enjoy the Morning* draws from the earlier fiction, but it does far more than the earlier fiction. It represents more than an accumulation of Kiely motifs and themes; it represents the culmination of them and a new level of artistic achievement.

If *Dogs* is the best of the author's long fiction, it is also the novel that is least understood. Although it was critically well-received in Britain, reviewers there suffering from a cultural myopia that causes them to attribute stage-Irish qualities to the modern Irish novel, experienced difficulty seeing beyond the farcical. The London *Times* critic labeled it, "Brothy . . . exactly what one might expect of a novel set in rural Ireland and full of bawdy, rollicking broths of boys and red-cheeked girls being tumbled in the hay and the whole thing tinged with sadness and drenched in porter and poetry." In fact what we have here is a farce and a laugh riot, and a novel that fairly bristles with hilarity. It is Kiely's most humorous fiction to date but, at the same time, his most profound commentary on human strength and human fallibility.

The farce is Irish, but it extends beyond a village along a Dublin bus route, a county like Carlow, Dublin, or Offaly, and beyond Ireland itself. Cosmona is aptly dubbed, for it is, after all, the microcosm in which the author plays out his human comedy. "All human life is here," he tells the reader, and so it is—with its full measure of sorrow and laughter. Paddy Kavanagh once noted that tragedy is comedy that is imperfect or incomplete, and in *Dogs Enjoy the Morning* the novelist from Tyrone has managed a magic blending of tragic and comic ingredients that reaches perfection in the higher form of the art.

Is it perhaps Kiely's intention to create a new fiction of the absurd where there are as many kicks as pricks? If the essence of absurdity lay in a kind of Beckettean awareness of consciousness, a revelation of man's tenuousness or the existential non-sense of being, then Kiely may be said to have transcended the mode entirely. This novel has sanity in its insanity, morality in its indecency, and religiosity in its irreverence. The miller of Cosmona tells the tale of the seven-foot giant who deserted the Prussian army, and who would each year climb to the summit of the mountain on the King of Prussia's birthday to fart three times toward Berlin. "If every man would fart at Kings, and fart at armies, and

fart at all brief authority," the miller asserts, "there
would be no wars except the sort of farting wars and
competitions they used to have in the County Kerry
in the olden times." In effect, Kiely's miller reduces the
follies and hypocrisies of humankind to a volley of farts
that are lost in the mountain wind.

But *Dogs Enjoy the Morning* has not been misread so
much as it has been read cursorily. It is at times as
"robust and gamey" as the *Punch* critic claims, and it is
even more entertaining than the *New Statesman* reviewer
makes it. But it is as if the critics have found all of the
comic reliefs without discovering the serious intent of
the novel; they have neglected to probe beneath the
surface and weigh the author's frequent philosophical
musings. "Everybody runs from life, nuns and monks
and hermits, and timid travelers who won't fly for fear of
crashing . . . ," he tells them. Whether the work be
regarded as mild satiric comedy or in the Saroyan vein
of the sentimental romance, full of comic and tragic
overtones, the novelist is earnestly conveying disap-
pointment, bitterness, and regret that the human animal
prefers to see himself in a glass darkly, that he takes
refuge in a mythos that is comfortably distracting, and
that his quest is a circular one that promises fulfillment
but fails to deliver.

Ten centuries ago the grey friars constructed the broad-
walled abbey with a high tower to alert them to the
danger of incursions from without. They called the place
of the abbey *Insula Viventium,* the Island of the Living, and
the local lore had it that no female of any species had
ever successfully penetrated their bastion of celibacy, . . .
but that was ten centuries ago. And it came to pass that

a village flowered beyond the walls of the abbey, a village that served a modern orthopedic hospital dominated by a legion of starched virginal nuns, a force of sex-starved nurses, and a pair of bawdy wardsmaids. In time, the ancient sanctity gave way to modern secularity, seclusion to seduction, and the island to the world. Cosmona was no longer a fitting refuge for Nicholas of Flue and other anchorites, or for fasting and flagellation. And it came to pass that the lethargic hamlet awoke with a start one day to find that the village idiots were having intercourse atop the sacred abbey tower with the whole world looking on. And it must also have come to pass that the preserved bodies of a thousand friars turned simultaneously in their graves, causing a tremor in the universe. In the gospel according to Kiely nothing is outside the realm of possibility; the outrageous is, in fact, commonplace.

The author explains, "This life was a game of consequences sometimes, and sometimes a game of comic contradictions, and sometimes the two mixed up together and a lot more besides." *Dogs Enjoy the Morning* has at its source the direst of consequences, a plethora of contradictions, and a creator with a talent for manipulating the consequences, contradictions, and "a lot more." He mingles past and present, pagan and Christian, conception and death, and he manages scores of episodes in piecing together a maniacal panorama. Sun-worshipping nuns preside over patients who are sometimes too much alive, and they distribute religious leaflets that cater to the holiest and most prurient in the same Biblical quotations—"He that loveth her loveth life. He that watches for her shall embrace her secrets."

The hospital chaplain is more concerned with banishing hares than he is in banishing evil spirits, the miller's strength is manifested in his son's infirmity, and the young cleric's pilgrimage to the tower is an ungodly quest. Even the pink walls, balconies, and coverlets mark the hospital's male ward, the blue the female ward. Is it any wonder, then, that madness vanquishes propriety with this "god from a machine" shifting the scenes and calling the tunes.

Cosmona is not Omagh. It is a fictional village, a composite of several of the author's favorite watering places, with one major artery, the ubiquitous Dublin Road, Ireland's own *Via Roma*. There is also a curious labyrinth of goat paths that wind into the mountain furze and twist back umbilical-like to the foot of the abbey tower from whence all village life has emanated. The paths crisscross the landscape and have the effect of throwing the characters into alternately calamitous and humorous situations that are so incredible as to be believed. And the principal village architecture is an asortment of geometric structures that span the historical spectrum and suggest definite sexual symbolism—an ancient phallic monolith associated with pagan fertility rites, the ruin of a medieval monk's tower (a truncated phallus), and a modern children's hospital in a semicircular design that insinuates feminine convexity.

The people in Cosmona are not unlike those in earlier Kiely novels, though it should probably be noted that the population is in no way typical of the Irish village, or of any village in the world. (One is tempted to punctuate that observation with a fervent "*Deo gratias.*") The Tourist Board might describe its inhabitants as gentry, clergy, doctors, tradesmen, and farmers but they run a gamut of occupations that defy categorization. The author is more concerned with assembling types for the proper tragicomic mixture than he is in representativeness. In Cosmona there are no heroes and no anti-heroes, but there is instead a humanity that is spread over a continuum of virtues—exhibiting various shades of courage, honesty, generosity, and understanding—and a humanity that is bound together by a common sexual obsession. Most of the inhabitants are local, though there are, during the ribald half holy week of the novel, four visiting journalists and a maiden from Dublin and a black sailor from far off Liberia as well.

The most engaging character of the novel is Gabriel Rock, the one-eyed, brain-damaged victim of human cruelty, who was "fathered by an angel." Gabriel is a cyclist *extraordinnaire* and Cosmona's man of mystery, whose nocturnal sessions quaffing Red Biddy, leering at suggestive book wrappers, and peeping up nurses' dresses from afar, catch the reader's fancy. Gabriel has suffered but Gabriel has also dreamed great dreams. He will break the world's cycling record from Cosmona to Crooked Bridge, and he will reach carnal fulfillment with the doctor's voluptuous young wife or a suitable facsimile thereof.

Gabriel Rock becomes Kiely's measure of human virtue and human viciousness, and even when he fornicates with Nora on the tower stage, he stands apart and above the men and women who seek the shadows and the ditches to perform the selfsame sex act. Gabriel's annunciation is, in effect, a revelation to the little world that concupiscence has made sinners of them all, but the

supreme irony is that Gabriel remains as sinless and
guiltless in the act as Father Jarlath's hounds. Human
pride and human perfidy drive the one-eyed angel from
Cosmona, leaving the reader to wonder with the narrator, what will become of Gabriel, the intrepid flier.

Growling Gabriel is not the only engaging character
in *Dogs Enjoy the Morning*. There are other inhabitants
whose madness, meanness, or eccentricities make them
memorable. Daft Nora, Gabriel's female counterpart,
skitters to and from the village pump until that inevitable
coital moment. (And it might be pointed out that it is not
the fact but the place and the time of the deed that spill
the coffee on the tablecloth.) Then there are the wicked
Cawleys who inflict misery on Gabriel and Nora, and
there is Peejay, a saintly dwarf of a handyman and the
self-appointed censor of Cosmona, who exposes village
debauchery to the world and who prefers the company of
his white cock to human companionship.

More important to the novel is Charles Row, a druid,
an historian, and a successor to the friars of *Insula Viventium* with the hereditary right of burial on the island.
Charles's cousin Grace describes him as "a mad professor
and a spoiled priest," and so he is. It is pedantic Charles
who sponsors the Irish *Lupercalia* on the mountain that
comes complete with virginal sacrifice, and it is druidic
Charles who reviews all the lore and legend that stands
behind the Cosmona triduum. The nagging pagan instinct that has the village in its grip has mythical significance in the ancient Feast of Lughnasa, when Pluto
came from a hole in the Blackstairs Mountains to
abduct a young maiden and carry her to the world of
shades, and it has added significance in the legend of

Cahir Row's den in Cathaoir na gCapell and Dark Domh-
nall, the highwayman, who has been confused with the
dark figure of the myth. But where does the pagan mind
end and the Christian mind begin? While Charles Row's
procession of hedonists and would-be hedonists wends
its way toward the pagan pillar of fertility, the confused
Gabriel mounts Nora on the Christian phallus, and the
black Liberian abducts a virgin of his own to reenact
the legend. All the world is in a kind of sexual harmony.
And through it all Charles Row proves himself the
worthy successor to the monks of the Island, for his
interest in mythology and history never extends beyond
an academic concern for liturgical and rubrical propri-
eties.

Cousin Grace's loveliness fades in hot flushes, as she
offers Charles a long-standing ordeal by cohabitation
and, if that isn't enough, she tempts him periodically
with fleshy London postcards and lingerie dyed an
enticing shade of red. But Grace realizes that she cannot vie with Charles's library or with his stone maiden
in the garden and, in hopeless resignation, she disqualifies
herself from future fertility rites. Cousin Grace can never be more than "cousin." She and Charles will go on
as they have, though the dogs on the street, the imbeciles
on the tower, and the stranger on the mountain can go
on having their fun.

The eighty-year-old Mortell is the only remaining
miller of Cosmona, St. Martin of the Mill, and the en-
during voice of sanity and compassion. Mortell's great-
ness lies in his ethical conviction based on a perfect
pagan-Christian syncretism and on his staunch Celtic
sense of independence. The miller is at once the grain

provider and the source of consolation to the entire village—to Gabriel Rock, to Peejay, to the Henafins, and to Stephen, his dying son. He confides to the chaplain that he would stand naked on top of the Moat to worship the sun, if he thought the people of Cosmona would understand, and the chaplain likewise confesses a faith in nature that should be tempered by Christian reaffirmation. Mortell speaks for tradition and the sacred values—for the time when the mill stood at the center of the community and when all men knew the miller and believed in him—but he realizes painfully that the old must make way for the new and that his mill must one day grind to a halt.

Cathy and Christy Henafin are destined to suffer through a lonely and loveless marriage; she with an attic of lifeless dolls, the memory of a ghost lover, and the shame of her husband's thievery; he with a fleeting vision of office, wealth, and physical conquests. The love of the sensitive barmaid and the dreaming convict cannot survive their expectations of romance and success or weather the years of physical separation. Christy's three-day visit is, as it were, an extended moment of truth for the couple. Cathy conceives a child and relinquishes her hold on dolls and ghosts, and Christy, the poet, quits Cosmona for a life in exile. There is pathos in Kiely's psychological examination of the Henafins and in his portrayals of Gabriel, Nora, Peejay, Charles and Grace Row, Martin Mortell and his dying son. In fact, most of those native to Cosmona seem to be victims of divine neglect and human rancor and, if they appear, at times, supercilious, ludicrous, or otherwise comical, the author suggests that they deserve more than a humorous dismissal.

The novelist is at his best, however, in his sketches of Dympha Cawley and Teresa Fallon, the fair maidens of Cosmona, who undertake that tumultuous journey to Dublin, a journey that has awsome repercussions for the entire village. In one hilarious episode they invest in sartorial finery, receive counsel from a taximan, a whore, and a "fashion model" with the exotic name of Amantha, and team up with an acrobatic African sailor with a voracious sex appetite. Ten miles out of Dublin, Amantha and the girls lighten the Black's wallet and abandon him. Amantha decides to accompany Dympna and Teresa to Cosmona, and the African, uttering "One, two, three, much fuck," decides to follow the trio and insure a fair return on his investment. Dympna Cawley and Teresa Fallon are Kiely's hell-raising country girls on the scent of excitement and romance, and he assures us that they will get more than their share.

Is there any hope for a Cosmona that breeds the likes of these? Is the author transforming the *Insula Viventium* into an *Insula Defunctorum,* or is he perhaps suggesting that God's castoffs might improve on the stock? Perhaps he means to better the breed by infusing vitality from without, by introducing a foreign element. Among the nonnative residents there are the Jaguar-driving doctor and his well-endowed wife, the young cleric on the mend and his pert nurse from Kenmare in Kerry, and Father Jarlath, "a shellshocked Finn MacCool," who has been appointed to serve as hospital chaplain. Among the nonresidents are the four Dublin journalists, Amantha, and the black Liberian with lust in his soul. *Dogs Enjoy the Morning* has a wonderful patchwork design and enough characters for several novels. Kiely superimposes scene on scene again, panning, fading, and blending

with the expertise of a film director and, while the stage of
Cosmona literally brims with activity, one never gets
the impression of overcrowding.

The young doctor is, like the miller, a humanitarian,
and he cannot avoid becoming his brother's keeper,
even if that brother is the flying angel. He defends Gabriel to his wife: "Gabriel's trumpet has caught us all
in the act," he tells her. "He's made Peeping Toms out
of the whole ruddy place." With a bit of luck the young
doctor may stay on in Cosmona; it is making a Christian
out of him, as the miller predicted it would. And Peter
Lane, the seminarian who is so fond of hoisting Nurse
Walters' blue skirt, has obviously come a long way in
resolving his religious scruples. Cosmona seems to have
made a man of him and a woman of his nurse. While
the rooks, jackdaws, and magpies chatter about how
much they enjoy the morning, the author insists that
Bishop, Deacon, and Martha, Father Jarlath's hounds,
enjoy it even more. The priest's unruly gundogs romp
through the novel unsanctimoniously threatening the
world of shifts and skirts (though it is Nora's terrier who
heralds the tower event). Jarlath himself has a simple
Pavlovian faith in God that he puts this way: "The manner in which, and the extent to which, dogs enjoy the
morning is one of the few things that have kept me
believing in the existence and goodness of God." The
world of sensations is an eternal Puck Fair, but only
the hounds and Gabriel and Nora have the non-presence
of mind to be fairgoers. Kiely long ago discovered
with O'Flaherty that "the birds and beasts are the
perfect children of the earth and, as a rule, the harmony
of their movements on the earth is disturbed only by the

invasion of man." To Jarlath and O'Flaherty, he responds a fervent "Amen."

The author's lyrical prose, witty dialogue, and vivid descriptions have been frequently noted. He is a magnificent stylist and a masterful storyteller, and nowhere are those qualities more evident than in this novel. His narrative flows on several levels simultaneously, not awkwardly and not strained. He uses literary devices effectively—"the Voice of God" from the speaker of the mobile T.B. unit on the Square that booms on demand, "You don't have to undress. It will only take a few minutes." The religious leaflets offer frequent consolation in droll ambiguities. The mural of *Treasure Island* whispers its significance from behind Peter Lane's hospital bed in the "playroom." Lines and phrases from James Stephens' "Goat Paths" sound the recurring background theme, and the reportage and commentary of the Dublin pressmen serve to unify and heighten the action of the novel.

Indeed in the intriguing imagery of Peter Lane's sexual fantasy, God is "the greatest goat in the world . . . in the center of a circle, buck lording it over a hundred black nuns and a hundred blue-and-white nurses . . . who all, nuns and nurses, chanted in upstanding medieval Latin that they were sitting on the bait." Peter is, of course, a Capricorn and that nurse of his is, naturally enough, a Gemini. He thinks to himself, "You offended God, and God was more likely, if He had any wit, to be up on the sunny hillside with the chewing meditative goats. The goats had their own idea of God: the strongest, gravest, most long-horned of the pucks who sat in the centre of the circle, no younger puck yet aspiring to the godhead, when the herd squatted to rest." In this novel God is unmistakably a goat, and the songs raised by Christy, who cannot help being a poet, and by the sunworshipping miller, and the Finn-like priest are essentially painful "goat songs," (tragoidia) that elicit sympathy and compassion.

What is it beyond storytelling that Benedict Kiely is about? Is the Cosmona tapestry only a rug of cartoons? Is the novel blasphemous, immoral, or artless? No, not any of those. What we have here is a satire full of Joycean barbs—the Dublin reporter's "Hic est enim calix," comes dangerously close. What Kiely is saying is that, if all human life is here, so is all human stupidity and cupidity and wisdom. Gabriel and Nora are exiled, Cathy Henafin is deserted, the miller's son dies, Peejay slays his wayward cock, Grace remains a withering virgin, and the black sailor is locked away in a dark dungeon. Meanwhile the "Ship of Fools," a great galleon of a truck with Christy, Dympna, and Teresa aboard, hurtles toward Dublin, the driver and his mate exchanging inanities with the passengers. These are the inexplicable absurdities of the novel and the inexplicable absurdities of life. What Kiely is saying is that the world needs more millers and doctors and priests like those of Cosmona, for even with their failings, they make the best case for continuity, and as the Monaghan poet says, "Continuity is everything."

Dogs Enjoy the Morning ridicules man's foibles and hypocrisies as it lauds his courage and his kindness. It says that men and women can move in nature's beauty and become worthy of the earth, if only they will curse the intelligence that has enslaved the spirit. It reiterates the author's firm belief that we are all mad, all murderous, and that we all hope for and need a particular and general salvation. As a kind of seriocomic parody on life, it falls short of savage satire, but it succeeds marvelously as a philosophical romance rich in myth and legend and pregnant in meaning. In his omniscience the narrator in *Dogs* also shows an understanding of the darkness and loneliness of Christy and Cathy Henafin and Grace Row and the Miller. The existentialism is unmistakable, but the difference in this novel is that there is more reason for hilarity and more reason to hope.

In *The Novel Now,* Anthony Burgess remarks that " . . . novelists nowadays do not care sufficiently or believe enough. Masterpieces spring out of conviction." *Dogs Enjoy the Morning* speaks the conscience of the novelist; it is his most convincing work to date. Burgess also says, "Any literate person with flair and cunning can produce a first novel of some sort; the test comes not with the second (which is expected to be disappointing) but with the third or fourth or fifth." *Dogs Enjoy the Morning* is Benedict Kiely's eighth. It establishes Kiely's claim as one of Ireland's important modern writers and ranks as one of the most outstanding contemporary novels in English.

6

Encore

In a recent review of a particularly bad novel, John
Broderick asked, "Why doesn't somebody write a novel
about real people? People who are not modish or chic
or so blinded by prejudice that they are only half-alive?
... Above all why can't I be allowed to review a new
book by that most potent wizard of words now writing
in the Anglo-Irish language, Benedict Kiely, so that I
might have the pleasure of praising a famous man?"
Kiely is not only the most prolific writer of fiction on
the current Irish scene, his novels are among the most
eagerly anticipated by the Irish. He is a writer of immense
talent and a writer whose work has grown in stature
over the past three decades.

There are those who would argue that it is his short
fiction that really matters. Frank O'Connor had good
things to say about *A Journey to the Seven Streams* and no
word for the novels. John Wilson Foster's "Dogs
Among the Moles," (*Eire-Ireland*, 1969) speaks to
Kiely's "brilliant evocations of rural and urban Ireland,"
his "sense of history and time," and "the harmony of
form and content" in his shorter fiction. And Foster
generously concludes that, in the genre, Kiely is "the

equal of O'Faolain and within hailing distance of O'Connor." Mervyn Wall also counts Kiely among the finest storytellers in Ireland today, but he does it without disparaging references to the novels. John Updike's response to the *New Yorker* stories, that they are "uniquely bewitching," is representative of the American critical purview. They are bewitching indeed.

But it is in the novel that Benedict Kiely excels and in the novel that he will be best remembered. The early novels move through the lush, green Ulster landscape and against the starkness of the Donegal seascape and inevitably gravitate to the metropolitan sprawl of Dublin. They offer plots that are more than acceptable, characters that are credible, and wonderful lyrical runs that lend a sense of wonderment to the scene. As works in the formative years, *Land without Stars, In a Harbour Green,* and *Call for a Miracle* might be excused for their failings, but each is a finished novel and each is enviable in its own right.

The later novels further develop the existentialism of *Call for a Miracle,* each offering a fascinating narrative variation. Donagh Hartigan's perversity is studied in the unraveling of a murder in *Honey Seems Bitter,* and the doctor challenges death, reenacting the plot of the Gaelic folktale in *Cards.* An eighteenth-century house in the Irish Midlands spurs faith and hope, while the house of the bewhiskered Captain at Bingen has a rank infectious air. In every case there is rejection of the positive good; there is loneliness, despair, intellectual barrenness, and the threat of annihilation. Kiely joins company with Hawthorne and Poe, Gorki and Dostoevsky, with Sartre, Kafka, and Greene. It is, however, in *Dogs Enjoy the Morning* that he introduces an element of comedy and achieves the proper cosmic balance. The novels are all commendable, but *Dogs* ranks as one of the outstanding contemporary English-language novels.

Writing of the Irish, Heinrich Böll said, "It is not good for an author to write on a subject which he likes too well." The novelist from Tyrone draws his fiction from a Northern town whose Gothic church has hopa-lo spires, from "an unbewildering city of a few bridges," from the experiences of an infirm seminarian and a successful journalist, and from Joyce, Yeats, Stephens, Carleton, and O'Casey, and from a myriad of sources that he loves all too well. Mr. Böll has obviously not read enough Kiely, but, then, we might all make the same claim. There are the eight novels and the thirty-eight stories, but there are many more to come.

Selected Bibliography

PRINCIPAL WORKS

A Ball of Malt and Madame Butterfly: A Dozen Stories. London: Victor Gollancz Ltd., 1973.

Call for a Miracle. London: Jonathan Cape, 1950; New York: E.P. Dutton, 1951.

The Captain with the Whiskers. London: Methuen, 1960; New York: Criterion Books, 1961.

The Cards of the Gambler. London: Methuen, 1953.

Counties of Contention: A Study of the Origins and Implications of the Partition of Ireland. Cork: Mercier Press, 1945.

Dogs Enjoy the Morning. London: Victor Gollancz Ltd., 1968; Harmondsworth, England: Penguin Books Ltd., 1971.

Honey Seems Bitter. New York: E. P. Dutton, 1952; London: Methuen, 1954. Also published under the title *The Evil Men Do.* New York: Dell, 1954.

In a Harbour Green. London: Jonathan Cape, 1949; New York: E. P. Dutton, 1950.

A Journey to the Seven Streams: Seventeen Stories. London: Methuen, 1963.

Land without Stars. London: Christopher Johnson, 1946.

Modern Irish Fiction—A Critique. Dublin: Golden Eagle Books, 1950.

Poor Scholar: A Study of the Works and Days of William Carleton (1794-1869). London and New York: Sheed and Ward, 1947; Dublin: Talbot Press, 1972.

There Was an Ancient House. London: Methuen, 1955.

SHORT STORIES

(Excluding those in the collections *A Ball of Malt and Madame Butterfly* (1973) and *A Journey to the Seven Streams* (1963), and novel excerpts appearing in periodicals.)

"A Cow in the House," *Texas Quarterly* IV (Winter, 1963): 39–49.

"The King's Shilling," *Irish Bookman* I (August, 1947): 33–77.

WORKS-IN-PROGRESS

"The Fairy Women of Lisbellaw"—a short story.

A Pictorial History of the Irish People—for Crown Publishers in New York.

"The Players and the Kings," a shorter version appeared in *The Lamp*.

Nothing Ever Happens at Carmincross—a novel.

A Question of Language—a novel.

APPRECIATIONS, CRITICISMS, AND REVIEWS

Since 1945 Kiely's criticism has appeared in more than twenty newspapers and literary journals. In addition to contributions to *The Standard, The Independent, The Press,* and *The Irish Times,* he has written for *America, The Bell, Books on Trial, The Capuchin Annual, Catholic Mind, The Ecclesiastical Record, Eire-Ireland, Hibernia, The Hollins Critic, Irish Bookman, Irish Monthly, The Kilkenny Magazine, Kenyon Review,* and *Month.* His commentary and reviews on Irish fare are regularly solicited by the editors of *The New York Times Book Review* and editors of special collections, like David Madden's *Rediscoveries* (New York: Crown, 1971) and Owen Dudley Edwards's *Conor Cruise O'Brien Introduces Ireland* (New York: McGraw-Hill, 1970).

CRITICAL STUDIES

Casey, Daniel J. "Benedict Kiely and Irish Fiction in America," *Aquarius,* Number Five (1972): 84–88.

Eckley, Grace. *Benedict Kiely.* New York: Twayne Publishers, Inc., 1972. (Number 145, *English Authors Series.*)

———. "The Fiction of Benedict Kiely," *Eire-Ireland* III (Winter, 1968): 55–65.

Foster, John Wilson. "Dogs Among the Moles: The Fictional World of Benedict Kiely," *Dublin Magazine,* Series 3, VIII (No. 6, 1969): 24–65.

———. *Separation and Return in the Fiction of Brian Moore, Michael McLaverty, and Benedict Kiely.* Ann Arbor, Michigan: University Microfilms (71–10, 721), 1970.

McMahon, Sean. "Books and Authors: Backgrounds for for the Study of Irish Literature," *Eire-Ireland* I (Spring, 1966): 77–88.

———. "The Black North," *Eire-Ireland* I (Summer, 1966): 63–73.

Share, Bernard. "The Corruptible Crown," *Hibernia* (June 23, 1972): p. 9.

Wall, Mervyn. "The Short Stories of Benedict Kiely," a radio script, R.T.E., 1971.